The Really Simple
Internet Guide

The Really Simple Internet Guide

John Morrish

Virgin

First published in Great Britain in 2000 by
Virgin Publishing Ltd
Thames Wharf Studios
Rainville Road
London
W6 9HA

A catalogue record for this book is available from the British
Library.

ISBN 0 7535 0501 0

Typeset by Galleon Typesetting, Ipswich
Printed and bound in Great Britain by Mackays of Chatham PLC

Contents

Introduction

The Navajo people of North America speak a language that is painfully difficult for almost everyone else in the world to understand. It's even more difficult than the Internet. Nonetheless, outsiders do need – and want – to learn Navajo. Apart from anything else, it's a challenge.

Years ago, a teacher wrote a guide to the language. He called it *Navajo Made Easier*, which was as much as he could honestly claim. This book offers something similar. *The Really Simple Internet Guide* aims to make the Internet easier. Easier, but not easy, because using the Internet is never going to be as simple as turning on the electric light, or the gas, or the BBC news.

The reason for that is partly that the technology is at an early stage, but mainly the sheer scale of the thing. It is not like sitting down in front of the television and choosing among five terrestrial channels, or even a hundred cable channels. People who have to count these things say there are at least a billion (in the sense of a thousand million) things to look at on the World Wide Web (WWW) alone – and that's only part of the whole Internet. To tackle the Internet, you have to find a way of breaking that lot down so it's more manageable. That's one of the skills this book intends to explain, with the result that you will no longer sit in front of your computer and feel overwhelmed by the sheer volume of possibilities.

Using the Internet effectively is about exercising choice and making decisions in a way that television viewers never have to contemplate. They can click the remote control from channel to channel, safe in the knowledge that they will eventually get back to where they began. Certainly no one is going to add any new channels while they are zapping the remote. But the Internet grows at somewhere between a million and two million items every day. That's at least a dozen every second – so that figure I gave earlier is already quickly becoming out of date.

Using the Internet is not as easy as watching the television, because it isn't a passive experience. The web might look a bit like television, but you can't wait for it to come to you, or you're going to be disappointed. But take note: the one definite thing we know about people who have got to grips with the Internet is that they stop watching so much television. It's no longer interesting enough for them. In fact, the Internet may be the antidote to television.

Unfortunately, a lot of the words used about the Internet give the wrong idea altogether: surfing, browsing, cruising. It's nothing like that for most people. Perhaps if you are an American college student with fast, free, government-funded access to a lot of local and relevant Internet sites, then it really does feel like surfing along on a sea of information or flicking along the shelves of a well-stocked library. Over here in the UK, it's a bit more like standing on a pebble beach in February: nothing happens for a long time and suddenly you're swamped with cold water. Or it's like waiting for the mobile library to visit: it takes a long time to arrive, and when it does many of the books are missing, damaged or foreign.

Luckily, these things are changing. The hand of British Telecom has been prised away from the Internet speed control. Most Britons can now get unmetered access to the Internet, meaning we no longer have to pay by the minute. And, if you can get it, you should. It's hard to see why a mental clock ticking up 1p or 4p a minute all the time should be such a formidable barrier to using the Internet in a relaxed, happy way, but it is. Trust me: once you know you can blamelessly leave the connection open while you answer the door, or deal with a crying child or make a cup of tea, your attitude to the Internet will be transformed. You can stop worrying about 'wasting' time on fruitless searches of websites and instead enjoy 'spending' time reading, writing and chatting to people all over the world.

On the other hand, just because we can now spend hours playing around on the Internet – and you need to do a bit of that if you are going to learn to enjoy it properly – it doesn't mean we always want to. The growth of material on the network means idly clicking around will get less satisfactory every year. Stay on the Internet as long as you're enjoying it and it's useful. Otherwise, get in, get what you want and get out. Nobody wants to spend hours staring at a screen when there's something better to do, such as taking a walk in the woods or playing with the children.

What you need to use this book

This book assumes that you have, or will acquire, some means of accessing the Internet. I discuss other possibilities, but you'll probably end up using a computer. They are still the best tool for the job. But every system is different. I don't just mean Windows 95 is different from Windows 98 or from Mac OS9. I mean the setup of every single computer is different. Perhaps when two brand-new Windows machines come out of the shop with their software preinstalled they are identical: but, by the end of their first day, they will be different, because their owners will have altered the software to their own liking.

When we come to discuss Internet software, the possible variations are almost endless: not only are there many different types of connection software, browsers and email programs, but they can all be installed and updated in many different ways. No book could possibly cover them all. I have tried to cover the general picture, with particular references to the main variations from the usual pattern. But it is your computer, and your setup. I make suggestions about the things you might do, and give advice about where you can get help to do it. But the book can't come round to your house, see what equipment and software you are using, and sort it out for you. You have to do that yourself.

In particular, I am assuming you know how to use the basics of the modern personal computer: that you can open and close files, handle windows, click on icons and drive a mouse. It would be nice if you knew how to create a shortcut or an alias, and how to install a program from a CD. If you can't, you can find a tutorial for either Windows and the Mac OS (Macintosh operating system) on your hard disk. And, if you bought the equipment new, whoever sold it to you has a clear duty to make sure you can do all those basics. If you bought it second hand, or you have somehow never learned those things, then anyone at all who has worked in an office in the last ten years will probably be able to show you how it's done. Or ask any schoolchild!

Beyond that, things get more complicated. Setting up a new or newish computer from scratch to use the Internet should be really simple. In fact it's *rarely* simple. And, if there are any complications, things quickly become incredibly frustrating. I consider myself a very experienced user of the Internet. I have been setting up Internet connections and email and Web software for many years: and it's still fraught with difficulties and complexities. In other words, I will do what I can, but don't be surprised if you need extra help.

Where to get help

Remember, if someone sells you something, it has to work. If someone sells you a computer so you can access the Internet, then that is what you have to be able to do. Similarly, if someone signs you up to their Internet service, then you have to be able to get that service to work. Keep that in the back of your mind, and your dealings with a whole range of unhelpful telephone helplines will be more fruitful. They are obliged to help you: they are not doing you a good turn.

True, you won't always have paid any money for some of the things you need help with. If you are using 'free' browser software, and 99 per cent of us do, then you may not feel you can ask for any help. But you can, and must: it might be free, but it's not a gift. Mr Gates has reasons for giving it to you and it is not only because he's a great philanthropist. Your 'free' Internet service provider (ISP) may not charge you for its services, but it is happy to claim you as a customer, direct advertising at you and take a cut of your telephone bill. Even a free 'unmetered' Internet service provider is giving you free access only in return for you agreeing to use its normal telephone service. In other words, you're a customer and as such you are always right.

So, if your computer doesn't appear to be working in the way it should, go back to the supplier and insist that you be helped to make it work: obviously, you can't expect much assistance if you have waited two years and in the meantime changed the main circuit board. If your browser software doesn't seem to be working, go back to whoever supplied it: usually your computer supplier or your ISP. You won't be surprised to see that Microsoft takes no direct responsibility even for Windows operating systems that have been installed by a computer supplier.

If you followed your ISP's instructions and you can't get your connection to work, then they must help you out. Don't be mesmerised by the thought of the £1-a-minute helpline. You are entitled to have a working connection before that pay-per-tweak system comes into being. Obviously, if they get you up and running and then you fiddle with things, then you have to expect to be plunged back into paying to have things put right.

Now, when you are first setting up your equipment, feel

free to use those helplines to the maximum extent. But that period of limitless free help comes to an end. The last computer I bought, a rather expensive laptop, had a ninety-day limit on free telephone advice. Not exactly generous. After that, you are on your own, but that doesn't mean you immediately have to start paying for support.

Windows and the Mac OS both have vast onscreen help systems. These can, in their different ways, be quite helpful, although not if your computer is so crashed that you can't call them up. In Windows, go to the Start menu and click on Help. You can choose by Contents (a list of topics), trawl through an Index or do a Search. Most of the stuff we will be dealing with will be under 'Connecting To Networks'. Click on that, another panel opens, and so on until you find some advice. It is not a particularly intuitive system to use, but there is a lot of material there, somewhere.

In Mac OS, you will always find a Help menu in the Menu bar. You want Mac Help, which has a list of topics or a Search facility. 'Internet and Networking' is the relevant topic here. The Mac Help system is more lively than that on Windows. It will open files for you and draw red lines round the things it wants you to look at and adjust. It also links to various 'Assistants' that help you do heavy-duty jobs. But, like the Wizards, their Windows equivalent, these can tend to bully you if you let them.

Of course, the relevant programs also have their own help systems. Internet Explorer has a Help item in its menu bar, full of lengthy and often baffling descriptions of its facilities. Netscape, the other well-known browser, has the same. So do the email programs you are likely to use.

The Mac OS also offers 'balloon help', which brings up little speech bubbles containing information when you place your mouse pointer over things on the screen. This is irritating but sometimes quite useful: it is the only way of finding out what every button and tick box on a control panel does, for instance.

The equivalent, similarly infuriating, system in Windows is accessed by clicking on the little question mark usually in the top right-hand corner of a window. That turns the pointer into a question mark. If you place it over an item on screen and hold down the left mouse button, some information appears. If you want to find out about something else, you have to go back and click the question mark again. On the other hand, you can often get information by pressing the right mouse button so that a box comes up saying 'What's This?' Then you click that with your left mouse button, and up comes a little message. No doubt there's a logic to it somewhere.

But what if you have had enough of automated advice, and yet you don't want to spend hours listening to 'Greensleeves' while you wait for someone to charge you £1 a minute to answer a problem that no sensible system would have allowed to happen? You probably don't want to hear this, but the answer is the Internet.

Obviously, you can go to the websites of all your hardware and software makers and of your Internet provider. They all have vast libraries of technical information and advice, and sometimes there are needles of wisdom buried in those haystacks of verbiage. Often you need to be able to construct a quite complex search to find what you want. If you take this route, take your time and be persistent. There's every possibility that other people have had a similar problem, and sometimes the manufacturer will even have admitted responsibility and found a solution.

But really you want human advice. The good news, however, is that you don't have to rely on the adolescent know-nothing pushing boxes at your local computer superstore. The Internet is full of 'forums' and discussion groups where people write in with their problems and other people solve them for nothing more than the fun of helping someone else and the thrill of gurudom. I won't list them all here, but, if you want to try a good British one, have a look at the site belonging to *The Times*'s Dr

Keyboard (a pseudonym, I suspect) at **www.drkeyboard. com**. He has lots of pages of standard technical advice, but, if you want anything unique, follow the links to his 'surgery', where he answers queries himself with assistance from other readers: **http://server3.ezboard.com/bdrkeyboard**.

You will have to register to use this, but it's painless.

If your web browser is causing the trouble, none of this will help. But, as long as you can get email or read a newsgroup, you can always find help in this way. I changed Internet providers recently and had all sorts of queries. But I wasn't going to pay £1 a minute, and the free 'email helpline' the provider promised literally never responded. So I searched around to see if I could find anyone discussing the service – I will show you how to do this later – and there were lots. Finally, I found a Usenet newsgroup devoted to nothing else (we'll talk about Usenet later). I placed my inquiry, got on with something else, and when I went back to look a couple of hours later my problem was effectively solved.

That, the sharing of expertise and experience for no obvious gain, is the old spirit of the Internet. After you have had a good look at the flashier aspects of the World Wide Web, the animations and sounds and video sequences, you may come to realise that the really important resource that the Internet makes available is people.

So try not to get bogged down in operating systems, browsers and email programs. The important thing is learning to use the Internet effectively. With that in mind, I always try to make sure I have two traditional tools alongside me when I am working on the computer: a pencil and paper. It won't crash, freeze or refuse to accept what I'm writing on it. And I will have a record of the really important stuff, no matter what happens on screen.

1   The Wonder of the Age

We are constantly told that the Internet is a modern technological miracle that will transform our lives. But for many of us that idea disappears the first time we sit down at a computer and try it. We expected something amazing, powerful, impressive and perhaps a little frightening. It turns out to be none of those things. It's frustrating, it's irritating, it's even . . . boring.

There is some truth in this, but part of the trouble is the nervousness people have about the Internet, especially those who don't use it frequently. Look at them: they are hunched and tense, their brows furrowed and their gaze fixed on the screen. They know they have to type something into the box at the top of the browser, but their fingers are clumsy and they type it wrongly, and nothing appears but a screen bearing a cryptic message. 'Error 404', it says. Did I type it wrong? Or did I type it right, but the thing I wanted is just not there any more?

So they try clicking the search button. A big page appears, rather like the contents page of a magazine but with things flashing on it. Somewhere in it is a box where they can type in their search. What are they interested in? Tennis. So they type in 'Tennis'. And almost immediately, the page comes back with the news that it has 1,895 pages for them to look at. It could have been worse, but which one to look at? They scroll down the list of the first ten, but there's nothing suitable, because what they really want to know is if there's a tennis club near them. But they choose one at random and wait for it to come. And wait, and wait. So they tap the Enter key (sometimes called Return) a few times, and click the mouse a few more. And the browser freezes. So much for the Information Superhighway, they think, reaching for the Yellow Pages.

It does not need to be like that. There are frustrations involved in using the Internet, especially if you are using it via your home telephone line. But it can also be incredibly useful and entertaining. The secret is to take a little time to work out how to use it. You wouldn't normally take a car and attempt to drive to Patagonia without at the very least acquiring a driving licence and a map. But the home computer and the 'browser' program are many times more complex than any four-wheeled vehicle.

And the 'network of networks', as the Internet was once known, makes the world's motorway network look like your garden path. There are no road maps for the Internet; there are no speed limits; there are no traffic police; there is no breakdown service. Why should you be able to find your way around, just because you have the means to travel?

Don't worry, you will. The more you use it, the more you will find your own way around, and that's the only way that counts. There is no right or wrong way to explore the Internet: it is simply a case of working out what you want to find, and going to get it.

The truth about the Internet, of course, is that you don't go anywhere. You sit at your screen and the world comes to it. And yet, while we happily accept that David Attenborough brings lions and tigers into our living rooms via the television, when we think of the Internet we always think of ourselves as going to it. Look at the names of the Internet browser programs: Explorer and Navigator.

So, let's not go against the grain. This book is going to show you how to go out there, get stuff and bring it back. It's a kind of handbook for the independent traveller. There are no package tours to the Internet. Perhaps there should be, if only to let people know some of the fascinating things that can be found out there.

So, without further ado, why not join me on a guided tour of a few of my favourite spots? They're all genuine, and I have given you their addresses so that you can follow my footsteps if you want. Otherwise, forget about computers and software and Internet connections for the time being and let me describe some of the sorts of things you are likely to encounter in an ordinary Internet session. While we travel, I'll fill you in a little bit on the history and customs of the places we visit and the habits and beliefs of some of the people who live there.

Leaving home

Imagine you're at home one evening and, amazingly enough, you discover there's nothing on television. Well, you like the BBC gardening programmes, and the last time you saw one of them you noted down the web address as it came up at the end of the programme. Good: if you have an address, or part of an address, always use it. Don't search unnecessarily.

So now you go to your computer. I actually use a laptop, so I can leave it around the house. I still have to plug it into the phone – although I could have a wireless connection if I could afford it – but it means it is accessible, almost part of the furniture rather than something tucked away and to be used only on special occasions.

You start up the computer, then click the icon to bring up your browser. I have my browser set so it opens on a blank page, but most people will be taken straight to their Internet provider's start page. So let's start with one of those: Freeserve (**www.freeserve.com**). The modem dials the number, with a string of horrible electronic bleeps (assuming you haven't opted for no dialling noises – see 'Control Panel(s)' in the Glossary for more on this), and we're there.

These start pages or 'portals' are designed to have everything for most of their normal users, but they try hard to capitalise on that. It's rather like arriving in a crowded bus station: it may be a good place to start exploring, but everybody there wants something from you and you'll be more comfortable once you get away. The noise! The people!

Luckily, we don't have to follow the crowd, because we have a web address, also known as a URL, or universal resource locator: **www.bbc.co.uk**. Let's type it into the Address/Location box above the big window of the browser. You may see web addresses beginning 'http://', but you don't need that any more if you are just typing into a browser. You do, however, need to type the rest correctly. As you are typing, you may see the address you want, or some variant of it, appearing in a little window that pops up underneath the address bar. If you slide the mouse cursor down, you can select one of those addresses instead, to save you typing.

Once you have the correct address in the box, click 'Go' (on the right) or just press ENTER. The existing page disappears, and the new one comes up, words first, then various coloured lines and panels, and finally the pictures. 'BBC Online Homepage', it says. 'Welcome to the UK's favourite website'.

OK, now what did we want? Gardening. First of all, move the scroll bar at the right side of the window so you can look over the whole page. Few pages are designed to fit within the postcard-shaped screen of your computer: they are usually shaped like an A4 piece of paper. You always have to scroll up and down to find what you want and sometimes you'll have to scroll from side to side as well.

Sadly, there is no big item about gardening. But there is no shortage of ways to link to a gardening page or two. On the left, a list of Categories includes 'Home & Garden'. At the top right, there's an arrow leading to an A–Z index. There's a 'Search BBC' box, too, but we won't use that unless we have to. Finally, at the bottom, there's a panel called 'TV and Radio websites'. Hold your mouse on the arrow beside it and a list of programme titles drops down.

So which is it to be? Well, we're interested in the range on offer. We don't have a specific site in mind. So we'll go to the list of categories and click on 'Home & Garden'. Nothing much happens, so we double-click, and the Home & Garden page arrives. Tip: if nothing happens when you click once, try double-clicking.

Well, the top thing on the page is a DIY project: an outside lounge. Pretty barmy, unless you happen to live in California, but there are some pictures of it, and an opportunity to see it in a 360-degree walkaround version. Ah, but to do that you must download some special software. How do you do that. Click where it says 'Download'. A new window pops up, telling you exactly what you need. It also asks your name and your email address, presumably so you can be sent some junk mail. Let's not bother.

But how do we get back? Normally, we'd click 'Back' on the browser. But here the button is greyed out. That's because we are in a 'pop-up window' that springs up to do this one job and is not part of your real browsing session. Click the tiny box in the top right-hand corner, the one with the little 'x' in it, and it closes: the gardening page is still underneath it.

At the bottom of the page is another little box with an arrow alongside it, containing more design projects. I'd like to see the thing about kitchen design, so I select that and click 'Go'. Up it comes. Well, it is pretty thin stuff, but it may be useful. Should I print it, or save it? I'll do both. To print, I click on 'Print'. Out it comes, pretty much as it is on screen. To save, I go to the File menu, where I have to choose whether I want to save it as text, as a complete web page called a web archive, or as an HTML-only document (HTML stands for Hyper Text Markup Language, and it's what's used to create websites – see Glossary). Other browsers will offer different choices, but here the choice is between the words, the words arranged as they appear on the screen, or words and pictures. For this we pick the complete web page, the words & pictures option, and press 'Save'.

Well, so far so good, but we haven't seen anything we couldn't get from a leaflet at the garden centre, assuming we could find one open at this time of night. What else is on offer on this page? Ah, over on the left there is another drop-down list of sites, and a list of underlined 'links' to other pages in this site. 'Chat' looks intriguing: what's that about? Click it and see.

Oh no! It's a long series of questions from viewers to an interior designer with long hair and a longer name. But up there on the right is something more interesting: an invitation to 'join in the chat on the Home and Garden message boards'. Maybe someone has some thoughts on the moss ruining my lawn. Click on the link, and another new page opens up. This one is very plain, with underlined links to a range of discussion topics. 'The Great Outdoors', says one, '389 messages'.

Let's have a look. The page opens, and there's a long list of subject headings with little comments or questions written underneath them by readers. Underneath those are answers to the queries and further comments, also by readers. This is one of the great traditions of the Internet: readers helping one another, rather than experts providing answers from on high. We could chip in, but we won't now because you have to register and provide a password, and we can't be bothered with that.

There's an awful lot here: cats; patios; thatching; knotweed; lawns; roses. But do I really want to read 389 messages to see if there's something about moss? I know, call up 'Find' on my browser (ctrl-F or command-F), type in the word and watch as all the examples on this page are highlighted. Apparently I should scarify my lawn. Perhaps I could email the contributor direct and find out more. No, that's not allowed in this message forum: but there are plenty of places on the Internet where it would be perfectly acceptable.

Well, that's enough gardening. How do I get back to

the main BBC page? Well, on any competently designed web page there will be a link back to the 'home page' or start page of the site. Here it is on the left, 'BBC Homepage'. But if I can't find that, I can always use the 'Back' button in the button bar above the browser window. That takes me back through all the pages I have seen, one at a time.

But if I hold the mouse button down over the arrow, the whole list of pages I have looked at recently is made visible: I can go straight to it. And, just in case that didn't give me enough options, I can find the Go menu or the Go submenu of the View menu (browsers vary) and select it from there.

Either way, I select 'BBC Homepage' and, a couple of seconds later, there I am. Oh no! While I've been using the Internet, I've missed the BBC TV news. Never mind, I should be able to find it here somewhere. There, right at the top of the Categories list on the left-hand side of the page: 'News'.

Click, and up comes a different start page. 'BBC News', it says, 'Front Page'. It looks like a conventional magazine contents page. But, as I move the pointer over headlines, it turns into a hand with a pointing finger. That indicates that the headline is a link, taking me to the whole story on another page. But there's more: a little picture of a camera with the word 'video' beside it, and a little picture of a loudspeaker, with the word 'audio' beside it. And here's one that says 'BBC One TV News', with a camera beside it. That's what I want.

I put the pointer over it, and the pointing finger appears. I click on it and another small window opens in front of the news page. This one is covered in elaborate controls and labels, but actually I don't have to do anything. A matchbox-sized picture appears, showing the familiar BBC clock: and there's George Alagiah, reading the news.

Well, it's hard to get too excited about this, because the

pictures are weirdly distorted and the sound seems to be coming from two cocoa tins connected by a length of string, especially when I can go back into the living room and watch it for real on the television. But it is clever. And I might feel more excited about it if I were somewhere on the far side of the planet and desperate to hear and see some news of home.

Note that the window the BBC news appears in does not look like one of the normal browser windows. It's not: it belongs to a program called RealPlayer, which pops up when called upon to help out the main browser by showing video and sounds. It's called a 'plug-in', and there are now hundreds like it. When you try to look at something that needs a plug-in, you will be told and invited to download it and store it on your computer. Usually it won't cost you anything, but it isn't particularly quick – RealPlayer takes about fifteen to twenty minutes – and it doesn't always work properly. Luckily, I already have that plug-in. We'll leave downloading until later.

So we watch the news, not live but recorded earlier. If we miss a bit, and we do because of 'net congestion', we can move a slider on the top of the screen and play that bit again. Sending video pictures over the Internet and then down ordinary copper phone lines is possible, but not particularly enjoyable. Evenings in Britain are particularly bad, because that's when the real Internet fiends in the US wake up and start bashing their keyboards.

The result is that the connections are saturated with traffic, and George Alagiah gets nastily broken up. Still, I like the idea of being able to get recent BBC news, so I will 'bookmark' the site. That means saving its address in my web browser so I can go back to it whenever I like without typing anything in. I do that by pulling down the 'Book-marks' or 'Favorites' (yes, it's spelled the American way) menu and selecting 'Add to Bookmarks/Favorites'. I don't have to type it.

Typing anything is to be avoided in using the Internet:

the things you type into address boxes have to be accurate, which they may not be if you are in a hurry. Mostly you navigate by links, properly called 'hyperlinks', which take you from page to page and site to site. Many sites will have a collection of links: some consist of little else.

On the news was something about storms on the eastern seaboard of the United States. I have a cousin who lives out there. I haven't seen him for ten years, but he was involved in electronics, so it seems very likely he'll have an email address. I wonder if I could track him down, somehow. I could just type his name into a search box like the one our man used at the beginning of the chapter when he was failing to find anything about tennis. I'm lucky that ours is not a particularly common surname. If his name were John Smith, we'd get nowhere like that.

Now I'm going to cheat. I know, because someone has told me, that there's a link on the Yahoo! page that helps you find people. If people give you useful tips, you should take note: people generally recommend only the things that have worked for them.

Now Yahoo! is the world's most famous Internet 'directory'. It's not the best, necessarily, but it is the best known. So I'm going to try typing 'Yahoo' direct into the address box and see what comes up. The addresses of big websites used to be really complicated, because people built their websites on machines belonging to big academic institutions. Now they own their own bit of Internet territory, called a 'domain', and it carries their name. So typing in 'Yahoo' would be a good start. And I know we don't need that 'http://' any more.

So I type just 'Yahoo'. And – what do you know! – the browser fills in the rest. I am taken straight to **www. yahoo.com**. Of course this trick works only with Yahoo!. If you want the Yahoo Riding Stables, Prop: L Gulliver, then you'll have to find a different way.

Yahoo!'s start page is another Internet bus station. Not many adverts this time, just a little banner at the top and a sponsor's logo at the bottom. You can click on these adverts at any time: they take you to the advertiser's site. But I'm on a mission, so I won't bother. Although Yahoo! is rich enough not to need a great deal of overt advertising, there is an awful lot of attention-grabbing on this site. Long lists of links, just like destination boards to places unknown. The big headings are for Yahoo!'s real business: they are the broad categories under which it stores all the web content its editors have selected. Click on one of those, and you'll find more subheadings; then click on one of those, and so on.

Remember those 'bookmarks' we talked about earlier? That's all Yahoo! is, really: a huge list of bookmarks started by a couple of graduate students in a trailer when the Internet was in its infancy. Now it's the biggest, most lucrative website of them all. And, because it brings people flocking to look at it, it has diversified into all sorts of other facilities intended to keep them there. Take a look on the right of the page: news, auctions, live broadcasts, email accounts. Or at the bottom, where it lists a lot of special-ised sites offering advice on everything from pets to banking and all the other countries where it offers local-ised versions. Including 'UK & Ireland'. Next time, I'll start there. I can place my mouse pointer over the link, click the right button (or hold the single Mac button down) and add it to my bookmarks without even going there.

But that's not what I came here for. I'm looking for a way of finding people. After scanning around, I find it at the top, along with Maps, Weather, Address Books, Shopping, the Yellow Pages and masses more: but People Search would seem to be what I'm looking for. One click, and I'm there. A series of simple boxes allows me to fill in my cousin's details.

Of course, it helps that I'm in the American Yahoo! I can search for a mail address and telephone number, and I can look for an email address. It would help if I had some more details. I think he lives in Virginia, but that's about it. I type in first and last name, and the two-letter code for the state (a link from the page tells me all those) and click 'Search'. A little icon turns up on the screen, either a spinning beach ball or an egg-timer, to indicate that we have to wait.

Well, what do you know? An address and a phone number. I can even, it says, 'click to call', but my computer is not set up for making phone calls so I don't do that. His name is underlined, indicating that it is a link. When I click on it, I am invited to click on further links to find what businesses are in my cousin's neighbourhood, and to be given a map. Well, why not? I wait for the map to load, wondering whether Americans can find us so easily. 'Not quite' is the answer.

When the map comes up, it is clear he lives right by the sea, somewhere between a big motorway and the raging Atlantic. In case I feel like dropping by, the map page also has a list of motels and gas stations. It's not terribly detailed, but I click on a 'zoom' button, and now it is. I can click on a printable version of the map, and the site will even give me driving instructions. Apparently 9.8 miles from Dulles airport, or 19 minutes. In this weather? They must be mad.

Should I ring him and ask about the weather? No, he'll probably have his hands full tying down his roof. I'll revert to my original plan, and find an email address. So I go back to the Yahoo! email search page, via the Go menu, and I come up trumps. I will definitely email him. Meanwhile, I can't help wondering what the atmosphere is like over there with a big storm heading their way. I wonder what advice they're giving on the local radio.

Actually, I don't have to wonder. I can hear their local radio. Internet radio lets me listen to radio stations from all over the world: they send their signals down the cables like all the other information going backwards and forwards. Like the Internet television, it's not perfect, but it beats short-wave radio. I could get to a list of radio stations in many ways. I could certainly find it from my browser's portal, especially if I'm using Netscape Online, which makes a feature of it. I could find it from Yahoo's directory, probably. But this time I'm going to do a search, using a 'search engine'.

It's a great name, isn't it? But really it's just a computer program that compares the words you type in with words in the documents it finds on the web. If there's a match, it points you in the direction of those pages. A search engine isn't the best tool for this job, really: you'd be better off with a Yahoo!-style directory. But search engines are interesting.

Pressing the search button on my browser takes me to the search system created or used by the browser maker. When you are more experienced, you may want something more powerful. But for now let's try it with Microsoft's search tools. I click Search on my browser's button bar, and a panel opens offering me various ways of searching. I click a button where it says 'Search for a web page' and decide what to type into the box. I want an Internet radio station in Washington, DC. So I don't type 'radio' or 'internet': I type all the important words in that phrase. I do this because I want a handful of pages, not 100,000. As it happens, I get 15,699, but I can be confident that the relevant ones are near the top.

A page of results comes up. Each entry is numbered, and has a heading and a description beneath. Number 12 looks promising. 'Washington DC's only all-news station,' it says. So I click the link, and arrive at WTOP's start page, which is not unlike the BBC's, but smaller. It has lots of links and a list of headlines: 'SEVERE THUNDERSTORM WARNING ISSUED IN NORTHERN VIRGINIA', it says. But how do I hear the station?

'Listen Live' it says, in a graphic near the top of the page. This is a link. Click it and RealPlayer opens once again, just as it did with the BBC news. And now my cousin and I are, in all probability, listening to the same local news on opposite sides of the Atlantic: it sounds like a rough night. It's tempting to email him to offer my support. But he isn't likely to be online now. Or perhaps he is. If so, we could chat straightaway.

As it happens, I have installed another little helper program, called AOL Instant Messenger. I don't actually belong to AOL, an online service, but that doesn't matter. There are lots of similar systems, but this is perhaps the biggest. I click on a little logo on my screen and ask to 'Sign On'. Previously I have signed on with the system's administrators. I have a screen name, like a nickname, and I have a password: but the computer stores these for me so there is nothing to remember.

The little control panel that comes up tells me which of my friends around the world is online at this time. But there is also a 'Find' button. If my cousin belongs to this system, and if he has given his details to its member directory, and if he's online, I may be able to send messages back and forth in real time. But he's not. What did you expect, a miracle?

Still, I note that another friend is online, so I click the IM (Instant Messaging) button, an open screen comes up and I type in a greeting. Within seconds, I get a response. Soon the banter is flying, as fast as our fingers can type. It's a bit like speaking over ship-to-shore radio, however, or an old walkie-talkie. Sometimes your contributions overlap. Nevertheless, it's fun and a painless introduction to what is called 'chat': here, though, you tend to chat to people you already know, or know of.

Well, that's enough transatlantic adventures. But before I log off, wasn't there something I promised to do. Oh yes, we're thinking of moving house, and I have promised to do a little bit of research about the area in question. Luckily, someone has recommended a useful site, with a snappy name. It's at **www.upmystreet.co.uk**. Saying good-bye, and signing off the AOL/Netscape chat system, AIM (if you don't, it can cause a lot of trouble), I open a new browser window and type in the address (sometimes known as the URL).

Up comes **UpMyStreet**, a commercial site that cleverly plays on several English obsessions. There is a box on the opening screen where you can type your postcode or your town. So that's what I do. Up comes a graph comparing the price of a typical semidetached house in my chosen location with the national average. But that's just the start: I can also compare the prices of different *types* of house, and I can choose a different point of comparison, for instance between my current area and the one to which I plan to move. But I can also compare school results, truancy rates, police clear-up rates and lots more. And, if you get bored with that, you can ask for a profile of your chosen areas, based on all manner of marketing databases. All irresistible, and precisely the sort of thing that only the Internet makes possible.

But I'm not supposed to be enjoying myself. The data on GCSE results looks worrying. A button on the site tells me about the best local school, but I want more detail. So I go to the main website of the British government, whose address I have previously stored in my bookmarks: **www.open.gov.uk**. Once there, I should be able to find the Office of Standards in Education, Ofsted, and find how this school is really rated.

This huge government site has, as I write, recently been redesigned, apparently by experts, and it is a mess. Still, you can find what you want. An index of organisations asks me to specify the letter of the alphabet under which the organisation concerned can be found. But I don't know whether it's 'O' for 'Office', 'S' for 'Standards' or 'E' for 'Education'. Luckily, a different 'topics' drop-down menu has an entry for 'Education', so I select that and click Go.

The next screen features a long alphabetical list of organisations involved in education, and Ofsted is there. I click it, and go to its own website. Luckily there are clear links to 'inspection reports'; and on that page there is a link to 'secondary schools'. And then another, before finally I can choose my education authority. The **upmystreet.co.uk** page told me that. Finally, I find the school and click on the link. But nothing seems to happen. In fact a 'pdf' file has been loaded on to my desktop. This is a special file that produces perfect paper documents, but it too needs a helper or plug-in program to work properly. Luckily, my browser already has that, and the file springs open before my very eyes. I prepare to print, but then realise the document has 45 pages. I'll leave it to read on screen.

Of course, most of this guided tour was just around the World Wide Web. Some veterans of the Internet insist that the web is hardly the real thing at all. As they say, no one rushes back from holiday to look to see if there are any new websites: but email is different. People really love email, especially once they explore email mailing lists, which provide a ready supply of stimulating reading matter and lively international discussion, for nothing, every day if you want them.

And then there are the FTP (File Transfer Protocol) sites, where you can download countless useful programs, fonts, games and software gadgets, usually for nothing or next to nothing. And then there are the 'Usenet' news groups.

The history of the Internet really began with FTP, sending files backwards and forwards, between government sites in America. The fact that the Internet has no centre, no organising body or government reflects the originators' idea that the information itself should be left to find the best way round the network. If one point on that network was not responding, either because it blew a fuse or someone dropped a hydrogen bomb on it, the information would just flow round it. Email followed, allowing the points on the network to talk to one another. But soon after that came the Users' Network, a way for people to have discussions and pass on news. Initially, the discussions were about computers, science and computer science. Now there are at least 60,000 of the so-called 'newsgroups' – discussion groups is more accurate – yabbering endlessly about everything you can think of, and a lot more besides.

So I'll end this guided tour by dropping in on a newsgroup. Remember, I wanted to know about moss and we looked at the BBC's little discussions. The newsgroups are like these, in that there is no authority figure answering queries: but there is also no one editing the commentary, vouching for their accuracy or keeping them within the bounds of legality.

Visitors to these wilder parts of the Internet are advised not to flash their money about or give it to plausible-sounding strangers, not to accept that anyone is necessarily who they say they are, and to be wary of giving away too much of one's own true identity. It is in these dark places that the original inhabitants of the Internet still live, and they are stern defenders of their own ways. The original Internet frowned on commerce, and in large parts of Usenet that still holds. The original Internet had no time for libel laws or censorship, and many Usenet people stick to those ideals, abused though they often are. The newsgroup folk can be impatient with newcomers, rude, chauvinistically American and self-interested. Too many of the groups are run by and for a hard core of regulars.

On the other hand, the Usenet crowd can often be learned, witty, thoughtful and generous in sharing their expertise. Many people think this is where the Internet really comes into its own. Not through flashy websites full of animation and clever graphics, but through people all over the world exchanging ideas and information for nothing except the sheer pleasure of it.

To go into the newsgroups, we close the web browser and call up our email program. The first time you go to news, it must download a list of all the groups. Just their names, you understand, but even that will take about twenty minutes. Then you must use the search box in the newsgroup window to find a subject you are interested in. I try typing in 'garden', and up comes **uk.rec.gardening**, which means a UK group concerned with the recreation of gardening.

Double-clicking on its name will open a program window for the newsgroup. Then you can ask it to download the headings on all the new discussions. Most email programs limit the number to about 300 at a time. When you find a header that interests you, click on it, and the article itself arrives. Nothing about moss, sadly, but an interesting item on *Paulownia lilacina*. It used to grow in the streets of Moscow, apparently.

You couldn't have a more genteel group than that one. Perhaps that's because it's British. Others are more wild and unpleasant: most of the horror stories about the misuses to which the Internet can be put can be traced to Usenet, as you will gather if you look up and down the list of groups. As the *News of the World*'s slogan used to put it, All Human Life Is There, and not only the nice bits. Later we will look at some more effective ways of finding your way around Usenet, so that you can find specific, useful discussions rather than a huge list of groups.

So, ladies and gentlemen, that concludes our brief tour of the Internet. Please take your belongings with you when vacating your scats.

Cynics have long taken the view that 90 per cent of everything is rubbish. Applied to the Internet, that would be harsh. But, even if it were true, the network is so vast that the valuable 10 per cent remains a huge and virtually untapped source of knowledge, enlightenment and sheer fun. But the only way to discover that is for yourself.

2 Making the Connection

So now you've seen just a few of the ways you can use the Internet for entertainment and information. But first you have to get connected.

The Internet is sometimes known as the 'Network of Networks', which explains it pretty well. Lots of organisations all over the world have large numbers of linked computers swapping information with one another. The Internet is really the high-speed high-capacity 'motorway' that links those smaller 'communities' together.

Just as you can't simply drive out on to the M25 where it passes your front door, you can't get on to the Internet without the proper means of entry. If you are working for a big organisation, that means of entry will be through the organisation's own network, which may already be linked to the Internet. If you are an ordinary person at home or in a small business, you join the Internet by using an Internet service provider, such as, say, Freeserve or Demon or NTL, or an 'online service', such as AOL or CompuServe.

These companies own the on-ramps to the Internet. First, however, you have to get to them, which usually means using the telephone lines, but could involve television cables or a mobile-phone service. The options are increasingly broad, but so are those for how you actually view the Internet.

You don't even have to have a computer. Already the first web-enabled fridges and microwave ovens have hit the American market. The Internet toaster cannot be far behind. Are there real alternatives to buying a computer?

Using the World Wide Web to its full extent means looking at a screen and listening to sounds. There are other parts of the Internet that are less demanding. You can have your email electronically read to you down the telephone if you like. But any method of using the Internet that hides its sheer visual gorgeousness is likely to disappoint most users.

Bear that in mind when someone tries to convince you that a games console, a glorified telephone with a screen, your television or a mobile phone is the ideal medium for using the Internet. They may not necessarily be giving you good advice.

What a load of WAP

Yes, information from the Internet can make its way on to the screens of so-called 'Wireless Access Protocol-enabled' (or WAP) mobile phones. But it is not the Internet as everyone else knows it. The screens show only fifteen words or so at a time: and all the time you are using the phone, you are connected at the usual mobile rates. The phones have access only to specially written pages, compiled by the phone operators from real web information. They are too slow to offer moving video or live sound. If you already have Internet access and you want something else, or if you must have the football results the minute they come in, WAP may have something to offer. But beware that this particular version of mobile Internet is likely to be replaced very quickly by something better.

A phone with a view

For people who don't want a computer, but would like some of the Internet's information, a telephone with a screen would appear to make sense. Several models are available, and many are in development. Amstrad's 'em@iler' and BT's 'Easicom' each cost about £80. They offer only email as yet, although there are suggestions that they will be upgraded to offer web access, of a type, through a limited selection of specially rewritten web pages designed to fit the modest display of the 'screenphone'.

They are unlikely, however, to be able to keep pace with developments on the Internet, because of their hardware limitations. They have no hard disk for storing the things you might find, and you are locked into a relationship with the one telephone company that supports them. They are the cheapest thing you can buy for sending and receiving email: but the deal with the telephone company means the actual cost of each email you send is surprisingly high. Amstrad's device also promises to bring you a lot of online advertising that you may not want.

But they are cheap, and very simple to use, if email is your main need.

Not just for games?
The Sega Dreamcast has Internet access built-in. The Sony PlayStation 2 will have it as an extra, possibly via wireless. Even the ancient GameBoy is to be fitted with some sort of Internet link. And, the GameBoy aside, there should be no problem with their technological capabilities. But they are not designed to do this job. And do you really want to drag the kids out of Tomb Raider 6 while you check your bank balance? If family money is tight, consider a second-hand computer just for the Internet.

Something good on the television: the web
You can now buy a television with built-in Internet access. The Bush Internet TV is a little portable with a fourteen-inch screen, a tiny keyboard built into the remote control and a connection to Virgin Net. It costs less than £199 and is intended to show that using the web is as simple as switching from *EastEnders* to *Coronation Street*.

Meanwhile, £100 will buy a 'set-top box' that gives your existing television Internet capabilities, plus an infrared keyboard to drive it. Web2U (**www.msu.co.uk**) promises full web access, and software that can be updated by regular downloads from the manufacturers. You also have to plug it into your telephone, of course, but it operates at the same speed as a computer modem. If you don't want to buy, a telephone company such as NTL (www.ntl.com) will give you a similar box in return for a promise to spend £10 a month on non-Internet phone calls.

For those with satellite digital television, Sky TV provides Open, not the Internet but its own shopping-based interactive TV service. A keyboard costs £35 to subscribers. ONdigital, the rival terrestrial digital service, offers email through its set-top boxes and a £30 keyboard, and says it will soon offer Internet access.

Television is not the best way to use the Internet. There is no hard disk in these boxes. You can't store much and you can't download programs to use for other home-computing jobs. You can, with some systems, watch the television in one window while flicking through the web or answering your email in another. But television screens lack the clarity of a computer monitor. They are designed for fast-moving fuzzy pictures, not stationary text.

Noncomputer Internet devices are considered in depth at **www.allnetdevices.com**. In the future, a new way of writing web pages is likely to make Internet televisions, fridges, toasters and vacuum cleaners much more usable. But for now, the Internet is designed for the computer.

What kind of computer?

It does not have to be new. Anything built within the last ten years or so will let you add a modem (the device that sends computer information down the telephone line) so you can read and send email. An old IBM-compatible PC running Windows 3.1, of the sort you see being dumped in skips, will let you look around the web. The same goes for an old Macintosh. The snag is that you can't use current software. However, if you have no money, but do have the enthusiasm to track down the necessary programs and make them work, this can be a good way of getting into the web.

Technically inclined friends – or your children (or some-one else's if you don't have any) – may be able to help. If you have a Mac, try **www.lowendmac.net**. For the PC, you should get help from a good Internet service provider, although some are interested only in helping uncompli-cated customers.

Originally the web consisted of pages of text with the odd diagram. Nowadays, many sites include pictures, graphics, animation, sounds, forms to fill in on screen and even video. These ask a lot from a computer, which means a modern machine is better.

But the web is nothing like as demanding as the latest computer games. That's why the computers in the shops are so powerful and why they have floor-shaking sound equip-ment. If you don't play games you don't need the latest and fastest of everything. A budget system will do everything most adults want. Spend any spare money on a good screen – and a good chair. You may be spending a lot of time in that position, and you want to be comfortable.

Incidentally, don't discount the idea of a good laptop. They have smaller screens, but you can use them anywhere you can find a telephone socket; or you can get a wireless connection. They make the Internet, and the computer, part of your daily life, rather than something locked away that you approach with a sense of duty. Sitting in the garden reading email is a surreal experience, but a pleasant one.

The IBM-compatible PC running the latest variant of Microsoft Windows is the straightforward choice. You will never have difficulty finding software, accessories or someone who claims to understand them. You also get a lot of beige box for your money, because their components are very cheap.

But you should consider the Apple Macintosh. Only about 5 per cent of computer users currently take that route. New programs come late to the Mac, if at all. It is more expensive than an anonymous Windows box, although no dearer than the top brands.

That 5 per cent, however, are enthusiastic and welcoming, as only endangered minorities can be. They will tell you that the Macintosh operating system, known as Mac OS, was the first with windows and the mouse and remains simpler to use. It is not the machine for people who want to tinker: it is a bit like buying a car with the bonnet welded shut. This makes it a productive tool and a good choice for home use, so long as you aren't obsessed with games, which are not the Mac's forte.

Windows, on the other hand, is endlessly customisable to your own tastes. The technically inclined like Windows PCs: they also keep a lot of technicians in business, because you can customise yourself into a lot of trouble very quickly.

When computers were about buying programs and using them, the Mac was an also-ran. On the web, however, no one knows or cares what machine you are using. Take a look at both systems and get the one you find more comfortable – or talk to people who have used both.

Be warned that a small proportion of Internet service providers don't accommodate the Mac, and that a few websites don't work properly because they require 'browser plug-ins', extra bits of software that are not available for that system. The glory of the web is that you can go somewhere else.

Whatever computer you choose, get the biggest and best monitor you can live with. The fifteen-inch size is now a minimum. You also need a CD-ROM for loading up software (many machines come with DVD drives that play CDs and let you watch movies). Finally, get as much memory as you can afford. You should try to get at least

64 MB (megabytes) of RAM. Memory is quite expensive, but it really makes a difference, whereas a few MHz (megahertz) on a computer's speed will not be noticeable.

Connecting to the Internet

The normal way of connecting to the Internet for home users is via the telephone line, through what is called a 'dial-up' connection. In other words, your computer dials the number of your Internet service provider or online service, you have your Internet session, you tell it to disconnect and the line goes back to normal telephone use. The speed of your connection is limited to the kind of speeds required for voice calls: which means it is not great for demanding Internet functions such as video, sound and downloading huge program files.

Now there are more options. There are cable connections, using the fibre-optic connections used for cable TV, which claim to work at ten times the speed of the normal phone line. And there are two new ways of hotting up the old-fashioned telephone lines: ISDN and ADSL. ISDN means having two phone lines and running them simultaneously to double or triple normal dial-up speeds. ADSL has the theoretical ability to run at forty times the speed of a normal telephone connection. BT is currently introducing a service that does not reach those speeds, is available only in part of the country and requires you to live within 3.5 kilometres of your exchange for good results. Nonetheless, it has great promise for the future. (See the Glossary for details.)

You may want one of these expensive 'broadband' services if you are a big user of the Internet, especially if you are creating your own sites. Most people, however, continue to use dial-up.

Using dial-up

This may seem obvious, but you don't have to have anyone's permission to start sending computer information down the phone lines. It's electricity, just the same as voice calls. It is assumed that you are using a modem that has been approved for sale in the British market. Unless you frequent a lot of car-boot sales, it will have been.

A modem (its name comes from the words '*mo*dulator' and '*de*modulator') is the device that turns computer information into signals you can send down a telephone wire. If you have a recent computer, it will have a modem built in. Current modems meet a standard called 'V90' and run at 56k, meaning they receive 56,000 'bits' per second. A bit is a single unit of data. It takes eight bits to represent a single letter of the alphabet. A modern modem can theoretically receive a single page email of about five hundred words in half a second.

Modems have reached their maximum theoretical speed: if you have a 56k modem, you can't upgrade it. If you have an older 14.4k or 28k model, however, it's a cheap way of getting a performance boost. But be aware that no 56k modem actually runs at 56k. If you get a regular 44–45k connection (this figure appears in the panel that appears on screen when you first connect) you are doing well. And all telephone modems receive more slowly than they send. Your modem will also allow you to send and receive faxes from your computer.

If you have a computer but no modem, you can easily add one. An external modem sits beside the computer. It is powered by a little transformer that plugs into the mains. Two cables come from the modem. One goes into the back of your computer. The other, with a normal BT-type telephone plug on it, goes into the phone socket on the wall. If you want to retain the use of your telephone you may need a simple splitter so you can plug both phone and modem into the same socket, or this may be built in; either way, you can't normally use both simultaneously.

Internal modems are inside your computer. They save desk space and are easy to fit, so long as you conquer your fear of opening the beige box. Follow the instructions carefully, or ask your computer dealer to do it: a big firm will certainly charge you. The modem is a long circuit card loaded with components. One edge slots into a connector, and the card is then secured to the computer case, with its single socket exposed through a slot in the back of the box. It needs only one connection, to the telephone, although some allow you to plug your phone into the computer so you can use it as an answering machine and so on.

Whether you are using an internal or external modem, you will have to make sure the computer knows it is there and can use it. Plug it in (into the telephone socket and, if necessary, into the computer) and switch it on. In Windows, go to the Start menu, then Settings/Control Panels/Add New Hardware. When you click on that icon, the 'wizard' – a program that guides you through various procedures – will spring up and tell you what to do. Your modem will have come with a CD-ROM of software: at some point Windows may ask for you to insert it. Do what it says. If you are using a Mac, you'll probably add an external modem, which plugs into the modem port (it has a picture of a telephone handset next to it). Then put the CD-ROM in the drive and then, after reading any files called ReadMe, double-click on any Installer icon you see. The software will tell you what to do next.

At some point, the software will try to complete the process by dialling a number and probably 'registering' your purchase of the modem with its makers. You don't need Internet access: it dials straight into the manufacturer's own line. Computers with their own modems will do something similar during the setup process.

If you ever change to ISDN, ADSL or cable, you will need a new box of tricks, not a modem but similar, to make the connection.

Choosing an Internet Service Provider or an Online Service

You can't get on to the Internet with just a modem and a telephone line. You need a company at the other end of the line to give you access to the Internet itself. The first choice is between an Internet Service Provider (ISP) and an online service: these, notably AOL and CompuServe, were originally private networks outside the Internet, but now provide access to the main event as well.

The distinction is slightly blurred: a lot of ISPs now provide a lot of interesting pages for their customers as well as Internet access. Nonetheless, their main job is to get their customers on and off the Internet itself. Both ISPs and online services perform other functions: they have computers to hold 'Usenet' discussion groups, and to hold web pages created by users. They also issue email addresses and hold your email until you collect it.

To pay or not to pay?

Just about everything you will want to look at on the Internet is free. There are some subscription sites that expect you to pay to look, but don't worry: you can't wander into them by mistake. Any site that wants money will make that clear by asking for your credit-card details before you can proceed. Most people find what they want on the web without paying a penny.

But all those computers and cables have to be paid for, and so does the bureaucracy involved in organising Internet addresses. These bills are paid by ISPs, by online services and by large organisations directly connected to the Internet. Obviously, they need to recoup those costs from their users.

When dial-up Internet access came to Britain, people paid two bills: one to British Telecom, for using its telephone lines, and the other to an Internet provider or online service. British Telecom charged a rental plus a charge per minute. ISPs and online services tended to have a fixed charge. This pattern is changing.

Those 'paid-for' ISPs still exist, offering a high level of service at a price. Their customers expect a good, fast connection every time, unlimited extra email addresses and free help and support at local call rates. They expect a generous amount of web space for their own sites, and easy access even from abroad. A typical ISP will cost up to £15 a month; increasingly, they are focused towards business users.

The online services

The online services, meanwhile, now number just two: AOL and CompuServe, which is owned by AOL. A lot of their activity is still generated by and for their own members: the services buy in a lot of content especially for them. They also offer controlled discussion forums on most subjects. They hold their members' hands when they get into difficulties. Some AOL and CompuServe members never bother with the Internet itself.

This is perhaps just as well, because the access they offer is not on a par with that offered by a good ISP, not least because they have their own software, which tries to make things simpler but can be slow, quirky and irritating. On the other hand, CompuServe has excellent dial-up facilities around the world, which makes it a good choice for long-haul business travellers.

AOL's way of charging is not particularly straightforward. At the time of going to press, it was charging nearly £4.95 a month for three hours' access. Any time after that is charged at £2.35 an hour, nearly 4p a minute. Or you can pay £9.99 a month plus 1p a minute. Neither is any great bargain, but access is via an 0800 number, so you get no call-time bill from BT. And there's no minimum BT charge of 5p per call: a penny a minute is a penny a minute.

CompuServe now comes in two versions. CompuServe 2000 costs £7.50 a month for unlimited use, and you still have to pay local call charges to BT. CompuServe 'Classic' is offered to those for whom CompuServe has yet to develop new software, meaning users of Macs and Windows NT. It costs $9.95 (approximately £6.95) for five hours a month, and then £1.20 an hour. You also have to pay for your telephone time. Why would you bother?

Well, AOL has said that its service offers the Internet with the complexities – and the frightening bits – removed. It is a 'family' service, with a heavy emphasis on games, sport and shopping. CompuServe, meanwhile, is now supposed to be a business service. If these things don't apply to you, you won't want either.

Free ISPs

When Freeserve arrived, it became possible to use the services of an Internet provider without paying for them. Freeserve and its imitators, companies such as ClaraNet, Virgin Net, UKonline and Madasafish, provide all the usual stuff: email, web access, web space, newsgroups. Some provide extensive content on their 'portals', meaning the home page they expect you to use. The result is that many Freeserve users, for instance, rarely venture into the rest of the Internet.

You may pay some money to a free ISP. Almost invariably, they charge for their telephone helplines: usually at about 50p a minute, which soon mounts up if you have somehow destroyed all your connection settings and need to be talked through them. But that is not how they get their money: they get it by taking a slice of the money you pay BT to use its phone lines to get to the Internet. That and by creating a large group of users who can be sold to advertisers. Most of these free ISPs are intimately linked with other businesses. Freeserve is owned by Dixon's, which means heavy doses of advertising for Dixon's, Currys and PC World. Paid-for ISPs don't inflict that on you.

Free-access and 'unmetered' ISPs

This is more like it. These are ISPs that not only waive the cost of their own Internet access services, they also get rid of the BT per-minute telephone charge you would normally pay.

It is not quite correct to call them 'free', however. As always, some money has to be generated somewhere, and in the most common version the ISP turns out to be a telephone company or to have a contract with a telephone company. To get the 'free' Internet access, you usually have to pay for something else. You may have to pay for an adapter to route your normal voice calls into the telephone company's system, and you may have to agree to spend a certain minimum sum on phone calls every month. Never mind: the important thing is that you now know the maximum sum your Internet use is going to cost you in a month, no matter how long you use it for or at what time of day or night.

If you sign up for a service with a minimum charge of £10 a month, and make £10 worth of phone calls, your Internet use has cost you £0.00. If you make no calls, your Internet use has cost you £10. Either way, once you know in advance that the most you can spend on accessing the Internet is £10, you don't have to worry about how much you are using it. You can use it when the mood strikes you, instead of worrying about what day it is, what time it is, whether bank holidays count as weekends and whether your ISP is one of your 'Friends and Family'. It becomes a basic resource like electricity, rather than a luxury like having someone round to wallpaper your hallway. No one wastes electricity deliberately, but at the same time no one gets out a calculator to find the most economical time to switch on the bedside lamp. Unmetered access takes a lot of the anxiety out of using the Internet.

It is not perfect, however. Some 'unmetered' providers allow unmetered access when it is cheap for them to do so: step forward BT. Most will sting you for telephone support:

£1 a minute in one example. All the unmetered companies have been, in various ways, swamped by demand. Expect to find it difficult to get service. They need you to use their telephone system: they don't much care whether you can get on to their Internet system. Remember, too, to take their telephone costs into account. finding exactly what BT charges is difficult enough, thanks to its absurd discount structures, and most of these new telephone companies make it no easier.

If you are going to need telephone support, take the price of that into account. You should insist on having a satisfactory working connection before the question of paid telephone support arises: ring the sales number, rather than the helpline, until you are happy.

You may not get a top-notch service after all that. You may not get through as quickly when your computer dials, and your speeds may be low. There may be restrictions on the way you use your free web space, if you get any. You are highly likely to be disconnected if you stay online for more than two hours, perhaps because you have forgotten. A nuisance, but not as big a nuisance as paying your phone company £4.80 for the call. Only if you regularly download huge files should it be a real hazard.

More seriously, you may be prevented from dialling up anywhere except the single telephone you originally nominate. This is bad news for 'road warriors', but the unmetered firms introduced it to stop people handing the free number and password to all their friends. This may change as, slowly and painfully, unmetered access becomes the norm.

Choosing an ISP

The serious way of choosing an Internet service provider is to study their performance. Look in something like *Internet Magazine* (**www.internet-magazine.com**), which provides the most exhaustive comparison tables. Ask your friends: most people use email, at least, these days and they may have good and bad experiences to share.

If you have Internet access already, or you can try it at a local library or Internet café, go to the websites of the leading candidates: find their prices, terms and conditions and see what extra content they offer. Don't get excited about free software: if it's free, you can get it somewhere else. If you know someone who is fairly clued up on the Internet, get him or her to help you look in the 'newsgroups' for discussions about UK internet providers: there were at least five at last count, full of unhappy ISP customers willing to sound off.

Ring your chosen candidates: ask about the costs, the price of support, restrictions on your use, and how they will help you get online in the first place. Ask if you can have lots of different email addresses: **john.smith@smallprovider.co.uk**, **jane.smith@smallprovider.co.uk** and so on. If you've got a Mac, make sure they aren't going to be unhelpful.

The relative importance of all these factors is up to you. After a while, most of them won't matter as long as you get quick, fast access when you need it. Most of the providers are less good in the evenings and at weekends, because people are trying to minimise their costs by using the Internet then. Unmetered access will ease that situation.

More noticeable than that, at least as far as the outside world is concerned, is the email name your ISP gives you. Ask yourself whether it has the image you want. There is an ancient prejudice about AOL addresses in the older parts of the Internet, the newsgroups for instance, because AOL is not considered the real Internet. Freeserve and Hotmail addresses don't look good in a business context, because they suggest you are a cheapskate and of no fixed abode respectively: you can get multiple Hotmail addresses in any name you like without actually having a computer of your own (see Glossary). And an email address that incorporates a comedy ISP name – **john@ravingbonkers.com** – might not look quite so funny when you are applying for a job as a High Court judge.

Signing up with an ISP

Finding an ISP is not hard. Any new computer will offer you several, built in to its installation software. A Windows 'wizard' or a Mac 'assistant' will dial up, take your details, and sign you up for at least a free trial with these carefully selected providers. They have, of course, been carefully selected because they were willing to pay for the privilege rather than on the basis of their service.

If you don't fancy being railroaded in that direction – one of the biggest chores of buying a new computer is dumping all that stuff – you can get ISP CDs from magazine covers, and from any number of shops, including Dixon's, WH Smith and Boots. You've probably even had a few drop through the letterbox, unsolicited.

I would be wary of loading up these CDs and giving them a spin. They often include programs to 'automate' the process of configuring your computer to talk to their system. Some of these programs fight to retain their grip if you ever try to take them off your machine and replace their settings with those of a rival ISP.

If you already have a working Internet connection, beware that these disks will try to overwrite what is already there. If you change your mind, you'll find it impossible to get back to where you were. They also load up their own Internet applications, the browser and email program, which may not be to your taste. Worse, they may destroy your existing ones in the process, simply because you clicked 'Yes' when you meant 'No'. You can lose all your stored emails, your address book, and your email account details. Reader, it happened to me.

If you have anything on the computer you don't want to lose, make sure it is backed up before you start fiddling with this sort of software. Look up 'backup' in the online Help system if you are not sure what to do. Then, if you want to proceed like that, make sure you have a bit of time in which you won't actually be needing to use the Internet. I'm sure some people find installing and reinstalling Internet software to be a routine task, but I have never been one of them.

In many ways, it makes more sense to install these things manually, the old-fashioned way, by opening up the relevant control panels and typing in the relevant details. At least that way you retain the illusion of control, and you learn something for when the setup goes wrong, as it may do. The special tool to use here is a pencil and some paper: write down anything you change, before and after.

Most modern computers will have all the relevant software built in, but it may never have been activated and it will need to be adjusted to suit your particular provider. Basically, you have to tell the computer what number to dial and what information to give the computers at your ISP, so that they will open up your mailbox and give you access to the Internet.

Windows and the Mac OS are now designed so that they establish an Internet connection as soon as you get them out of the box and plug them in, with the help of our old friends the wizard and the assistant.

In Windows, find the Internet Connection Wizard, either on the desktop or by following these steps: Start/Programs/Accessories/Communications. When you get there you should see the icon for the Wizard: disappointingly, it is not wearing a pointy hat, but it does have its name on it. Open it.

Now you can decide whether you want: a new Internet account; your existing account (if you have one) moved to this machine; or just to be left to configure things manually. If we want a new account, click on the button beside that option, then on Next. Before you know it a message appears to tell you it is dialling Microsoft's 'Internet Referral Service'. You will probably hear the usual horrible row of a modem dialling and connecting. If it doesn't work, click the box to try again. If that doesn't work, ring whoever sold you the machine and tell them you have trouble. At this stage, it is their responsibility.

You probably won't have any trouble. Sooner or later, a new panel will appear on screen with a list of likely providers. You can click an arrow to browse through their details. Pick one if you want. A form appears, asking for your name, address and telephone number. Type them in: using the Internet involves a lot of form filling, so you might as well get used to it. If you get something wrong, you can delete and do it again. When you are happy, click Next.

Now you get some information. Did you know that the 'free' ISP you selected expects £5.99 a month for technical support? Click Next and you will be taken to a form asking for your credit-card details. Now you must confirm you want to join. If not, click Cancel.

But you clicked Next, which is Windows-speak for Yes. Now Windows adjusts all your control panels and dials the provider's phone number. Now you're in the sign-up area: you are asked to suggest your own email 'username'. That's the bit before the '@'. You do not have to use your real name or even anything like it: but most of us find our real names have their uses. The form also asks for a 'security word' that will identify you as you if you have to call the ISP's staff. Click Next and a lengthy membership agreement appears. You should read it carefully. No, you really should.

Click Next, and a whole series of details appear. Write them down using that well-known, nonvolatile method of storage we call paper. They include your password: your computer should record it, but it may decide not to. And now you must sign up, or withdraw. If you sign, Windows makes a lot of noise writing things to its hard disk, then asks if you'd like to connect to your new account. At which point it dials, opens your new browser (probably Internet Explorer) and takes you to the ISP's start page. It will also have configured your email program, too. You'll find that on your desktop, and if you ask to check your mail you'll find you have a nice welcome message from

Microsoft and from your ISP. You can write a message, by selecting 'New Message' in the File menu, and it will have your new email address already in the 'From' box. You are now online. Easy, wasn't it?

Turning briefly to the Mac, the automatic helper you want for the same job is called Internet Setup Assistant. If you need to find a new provider, he will bring in his friend the ISP Info Assistant. If you have a provider already, or you want to use one who is not available through the Assistant (and the selection is feeble), you will need to gather various bits of information and fill them in yourself: see the section on connecting manually. Otherwise, the process is similar to the Windows system described above, but you tend to have to answer Yes or Cancel instead of clicking Next.

Using a CD-ROM to connect to an ISP

First, get an Internet-connection CD-ROM from a magazine or a shop or directly from the ISPs. Be wary of AOL's CD unless you actually want to join AOL. It will do that job, but it will not help if you change your mind later. Place it in the CD drive and watch what happens. It may well open up straightaway. If it doesn't, find it: it's drive D in My Computer in Windows, or it will be on the desktop in Mac.

You may now see a folder full of little folders and icons. Find the one with the right name – 'Join RavingBonkers. com', for instance – and click it. Alternatively, you may be in a sort of magazine page or glossy advertisement and may have to hunt around for the icon or button that will start the installation. If it's a free ISP, by the way, you probably won't be asked for your credit-card details, but you will be asked all sorts of things. Sainsbury's will want your 'loyalty card' number, for instance.

Now the installer software asks if you would like a browser/email package installed or just Internet access. If you have a working browser, say no to that. You can always install the new one later. If you have an older browser and you haven't got it working, then by all means say yes to the new one. Otherwise, click the button that says 'Register'. The software dials, and launches your browser, new or old, and now a series of forms appears, asking for your phone number, name, address and so on. This time, you may be asked to choose your own password as well as your 'security word' and email username. If your chosen username is 'jsmith', don't be surprised that someone will already have it: the ISP can't accommodate two people with the same username. A new one will be suggested: probably 'j_smith117' or something equally memorable, but you don't have to use it. You can usually do better, bearing in mind that you want to be able to tell people about it over the phone. In the end, when the ISP's computer accepts one of your suggestions, you will be told to write it down.

Next you will have to choose between making this ISP 'your ISP', installing it while leaving your existing email and news settings as they were, and making your connections manually. Choose the first if you have no existing ISP or if you are certain that you don't want to use that one any more. Any outgoing email will now come from your new ISP's address, and you will go straight there when you connect, to get your email and read newsgroups. But choose the second option if you want to keep both accounts open, giving you a choice of email addresses. With luck it will stop the installation process wiping out all your previous connections.

The third, manual, option might seem the most complicated, but it has a lot in its favour. It takes you to a page full of the information you need to configure the system. If you can print it, do so, otherwise write it down. These numbers and codes should ensure you can keep the pricey telephone helpline at bay in future.

If you take one of the automatic options, you should now go rapidly to your new ISP's start page, where you will discover what you have signed up for. If things have not been set up to your taste – a password you don't like, the wrong security word – you can usually change them. The only tricky one with some ISPs is the username: once you've agreed to that, you may be stuck with it.

Connecting manually to an ISP

You may not be able to connect to your chosen ISP with a CD, or may prefer not to. Mac users, particularly, have to become adept at configuring their own connections in a Windows-based world. Some ISPs may not like supplying the information for you to sign up like this, but that's just for their administrative convenience. Try a different one.

Some will have the information on a sheet of paper, which they will send or fax you. Others will have it on their website. Once you have access to a working Internet connection, you can easily find and join an ISP online.

On any ISP's website, you will find a link saying something like 'Join now!' That leads you to a form, where you will be asked the usual details. Sometimes they also like to know where you heard about them. Then it asks you to try creating an email address for yourself, using a special form containing a blank space followed by the provider's name. Like this: [blank]@smallprovider.co.uk. So you try your name: johnsmith@smallprovider.co.uk. Someone has it, so you try again until you arrive at jsmith3@smallprovider. co.uk. On the same form, you choose a password, typing it twice to confirm. Passwords should really have a combination of letters and numbers, and should not be real words: unfortunately, those are the only words most of us can remember.

Now a new screen appears, telling you your account details. Print them or write them down, because they are everything you need to configure your computer to use this ISP. You may even find a button to configure things automatically, but only if you are using Windows and

Internet Explorer. If you're not doing that, close your browser and close your Internet connection.

Once you've got that piece of paper, whether by web or by post, you are in business. Set aside a good hour, make sure you're not disturbed, and restart your computer. Setting up an Internet connection is not exactly fun, but it is rewarding when you get it right.

This is the process in Windows. Go to Start/Accessories/Communications and find an icon called Dial Up Networking. Open it, and find an icon called Make New Connection. Double-click it, and up comes the first of many panels you have to fill in. Where it says 'the computer you are dialling', type the ISP's name. Ignore the stuff about modems, unless you've got more than one, and click Next. Now type in the dialling code and the number your ISP has told you to use: it will probably be an 0845 number for normal 'local call rate' access, or 0800 if it is an unmetered ISP. Click Next and then Finish.

You will be back at the Dial-Up Networking panel, which now has an icon representing your new connection, with the name you gave it underneath. Click on it with your right button, then select Properties from the menu that appears.

A new panel appears. Make sure the box about using area code has a tick by it. If not, click it. Now click the tab or button that says 'Server Types'. On the panel that opens, only the box marked TCP/IP should have a tick. Now click on 'TCP/IP settings' to open another panel.

Here both 'Server assigned IP address' and 'Server assigned name server addresses' should be ticked. Leave everything else alone. Click OK to close the panel, and then close the one that appears next. You are now back with the Dial-Up Connections window.

This time, double-click on the icon for your new ISP. Enter the username and password that you were given when you signed up. The account username may not be the same as your email username: some ISPs prefer to issue a meaningless string of characters. But at least you can tick the box and ask Windows to save your password.

Now, click Connect and hear your modem dial up. A panel appears on screen with an animation of a signal passing between two computers. When a successful connection is made, a bigger panel appears to tell you that you are connected and offers more information: actually, it doesn't tell you much. All the time you are connected, an icon of two computers will appear in the bottom right corner of your screen, next to the clock. Click on that icon if you want to disconnect.

Manual connection with the Mac

Internet connections are tricky on older Macs, but anything using OS8 or later shouldn't present too many problems. Open the Apple menu and find Control Panels. You want PPP in OS8 or Remote Access in OS9. They are effectively the same thing.

Open the panel, then go to the File menu and select Configurations. In the panel that appears, select Default by highlighting it. Now click Duplicate: this gives you a spare set of configurations you can fiddle with without destroying your originals. Type the ISP's name (say 'Smallprovider') into the box that appears. Now all the settings are revealed for you to adjust: you can go back to the originals just by selecting Default in the Configurations panel.

If no settings are visible in the new Smallprovider panel, you can bring them out by clicking the little triangle on the left. Ensure the Registered User button is selected, then write your new username into the 'Name' box. Now comes the password you agreed with your ISP. It must be exactly as originally written, with any capital letters in place. You should click the 'Save password' box, for convenience, but you should write the password down somewhere safe as well. Finally, type in the telephone number you were given.

Now, click on the Options button. A panel appears

with three tabs along the top. The first controls redialling. Don't choose too many redials: the Mac is frozen while the process takes place. The second controls what happens during connection. Click the box for 'Flash icon in menu bar': this is the only way you will have of telling whether you are online or not. Put a number in the 'Disconnect if idle for . . .' box. Most people put ten minutes or so. It doesn't matter, moneywise, if you have an unmetered ISP – but what if people are trying to telephone you? This way you can do a long download and leave the computer to disconnect itself at the end without your having to stand over it.

In PPP, the OS8 version of this panel, you also specify here whether you want your browser and email programs ('TCP/IP applications') to connect automatically when they start. This is a nuisance if, like most of us in Britain, you prefer to work on your emails off-line before sending them. In OS9 you will find that choice moved to the final tab: 'Protocol'.

In the 'Protocol' panel you might click the boxes and 'Allow error correction' or 'Use TCP header compression': neither seems to make much difference. Now click OK, the Options panel will close and you will be back in PPP/Remote Access. Close it, and you will be asked if you want to save your changes. You do. Now you can reopen the panel and click Connect. The panel will tell you it is connecting, the speed at which it has connected and how long you have been connected. All the time the connection is open, a little telegraph pole icon flashes alternately with the Apple on the Apple menu. For practical purposes, you may well want to create an alias to this control panel so you can get at it easily. Or use Control Strip: details are in the built-in Mac Help system.

How to disconnect

Many Internet beginners worry that they will start a connection, find some interesting foreign-based page, and then be unable to close the connection, leading to a telephone bill the size of the national debt. Luckily, this is unrealistic. Even a paid-for ISP will normally charge you only local call rates: if you can't dial up at local rates from wherever you need to be, get a different provider.

Still, you do need to know how to disconnect. Windows has a feature called 'auto-disconnect' which, typically, doesn't do that at all. You might think it would cut you off when you close your browser. Instead, when you close the last Internet-related window on your screen, it triggers a pop-up menu suggesting you disconnect, with a button saying exactly that. If you don't click it, it doesn't do anything immediately but gently disconnects you after the number of minutes you have set in the 'Disconnect if idle for [blank] minutes' box in a panel called Advanced Dial-Up. You find that like this: Start/Settings/Control Panels/Internet Options or by choosing Internet Options in Internet Explorer. Once in the Internet Options panel, click Connections, then Settings and finally Advanced. That brings you to the Advanced Dial-Up panel, where you click beside 'Disconnect when connection may no longer be needed' to set up the 'auto-disconnect warning' as well as setting the delay before disconnection takes place. Beware: the computer does not register activity if you are not actually clicking anything on screen. Set the delay time too low and it may disconnect you while you are still reading something. Try ten to twenty minutes.

If you don't use 'auto-disconnect', you can close your browser or email program and leave the connection running with no indication except the little icon in the task bar. Right-click (click the right-hand button) or double-click it to bring up a disconnect button.

Disconnect the Mac by using the Remote Access or PPP panels or an alias. You may also have an item called 'Connect to the Internet' in the Apple menu which has a 'Disconnect' button when you are connected. Some Mac email programs will disconnect the Internet connection when they have collected new mail. Web browsers can connect automatically, but do not disconnect when you close them.

You can disconnect your computer at any time: you don't have to wait for your browser or email program to close. If the browser freezes when a page won't load, you can disconnect; but the browser may try to dial up again to finish the job it was doing. At the very least, click the browser's Stop button if you can. If the browser crashes and your pointer freezes, try to quit the program from the keyboard. Failing that, press CTRL-ALT-DEL in Windows or command-option-esc in the Mac. That may close the program and give you back the mouse, while leaving the Internet connection running. If the computer freezes altogether, you will have to do what you can to restart. Try to avoid having to use the power switch for this in Windows, or the dreaded 'paperclip' restart button in modern Macs. But, if you restart, your Internet connection will definitely be broken, as it will be if you pull the plug out of the wall. If you can hear a dialling tone when you pick up the telephone on the same line, the connection is broken.

So, now you know how to connect to the Internet, and, just as importantly, you know how to disconnect. Now it's time to do something a little bit more exciting.

3 Let's Go Surfing

Everybody's learning how – except that a lot of people are doing it without learning. It really is that straightforward, but a few hints can help make it much easier for you to get what you want from the Internet.

You now have a working Internet connection. But to do anything at all, you need software. Luckily, it all comes these days in one or two huge packages. There is your web browser, usually Internet Explorer or Netscape (also known as Navigator or Communicator). And there is your email program, usually Outlook Express or Netscape Messenger. Netscape treats browsing and email as parts of the same overall program: Microsoft treats them as separate entities.

You probably have these programs already: they have been 'bundled' with new computers for at least the last five years. If you have had them and haven't used them, they may benefit from being upgraded. That won't cost you anything: these programs are provided free.

Which means that if you don't have them, you can get them on the cover disk of just about any monthly computer or Internet magazine. Or you can download them from the Microsoft and Netscape websites, if you have a working web setup. But try not to do that: it will take you at least an hour in each case.

We'll look at email programs later. For now, let's consider web browsers. The browser does two basic jobs: it makes it possible for you to connect to web sites, and it displays the material you find there. They should perhaps be called web grabbers or web suckers, because they find stuff and bring it to you. You don't go anywhere. But that's not a very exciting image, so instead the browsers project an image of adventure: we use them to explore and to navigate. Without leaving our desks.

This may seem a banal observation, but many Internet beginners worry on a less-than-conscious level that they will be transported somewhere they don't like and won't be able to get back. So when they can't get to a particular page, and the browser freezes, they wonder whether they are somehow trapped in limbo. More to the point, they wonder whether their phone is still connected, which might be costing them money.

If this happens to you, don't panic. Lift the phone off the hook and listen: you do connect via a two-way splitter, don't you? If you hear a dialling tone, you're not connected. If you hear electronic bleeps and a sound like rushing wind, then you are.

If you find yourself somewhere you don't like, you can reverse your steps using the browser controls, or you can close the window. If that doesn't work, or closing the window brings up another window, and then another (a website programmers' trick that should be outlawed), you can quit the browser itself. You may be asked if you want to close your connection now. You can if you want. But if your windows won't close, and your browser won't quit, and your pointer won't move, what can you do then? Force it to quit, using CTRL-ALT-DEL in Windows (I don't believe you've never had to do that) or command-option-esc in Mac OS. And if that doesn't work close down the operating system and restart: CTRL-ALT-DEL again in Windows, hold down the power button in Mac. At this point, pick up the phone again: you will have disconnected. That's the last resort: it's good to know it before you start. You cannot stay connected if your computer doesn't actively remind the telephone system that it's still here.

Which browser?

For most new users of the web, it really doesn't matter. When you are more experienced, you'll develop ideas about what you need, and then you can choose between the options. Netscape was the first commercial browser. It's looking a bit dated but it does the basics pretty well. A new version, Netscape 6, is – at the time of writing – promised soon. It may even be around by the time you read this. It will look nicer. Most likely, you will have Internet Explorer on your computer, and many of your friends and colleagues will be using it: that's good, because you can ask them for help. It has been updated more recently than Netscape and has all sorts of odd new features: an auction manager, for instance. It has one thing that sets it apart: it will save whole web pages, even whole sites, with their pictures and drawings in the right places, with one click. Netscape won't do that: you have to save the words and page layout with one click, and then all the pictures one by one.

Microsoft also claim their browser does the best job of accurately meeting all the established standards for web design: in other words, pages look the way they should. Certainly, they look different from the way they look on Netscape.

Is either browser quicker or more reliable? That depends much more on the way you have your machine set up than on their own inherent qualities. People argue it both ways. If you want a really fast, stable browser, you might do better to pay for one, with real money, from one of the independent software companies who have ventured into the market recently. See 'browsers' in the Glossary.

These are incredibly complex programs. There are countless options for adjusting both the way they bring in pages and the way they display, save and print what they have found. Better to get to know one browser, perhaps, before hankering after others.

So, check to see if you have a browser on your machine.

It should be obvious: there will be an icon on the desktop, on the taskbar, on the Start menu or (in Mac) in the Apple Menu. If you've bought an old machine, the previous owner may not have used it, so it may be buried in a folder somewhere. Use the Find . . . system, typing in 'Explorer' or 'Navigator'. Beware: Internet Explorer is different from Windows Explorer, despite the similarity in their names – why did they do that?

If you really can't find it, you'll have to install or reinstall a browser from scratch. Get a CD from somewhere: your ISP will usually supply one, or your local supermarket, or any computer magazine. Better this than a downloaded file you could accidentally erase. You've probably got some browser CDs lying around that you haven't noticed. Drop it into the tray, or the slot, and start the process.

As you go, be a little bit careful. If you have a working Internet connection, loading up a new browser may damage your old settings. You should back up everything important first, although you probably won't. At the very least, back up everything to do with that connection, particularly your email files if you are already using email. If you're doing it all for the first time, there is less to worry about. You can't damage an Internet connection that doesn't exist.

The installation process

Now this should be simple, but it is much easier to do than to explain, because every combination of browser, operating system and computer installs things slightly differently. It even matters where you got the CD: a magazine will wrap the software up in a kind of magazine page; a supermarket might hide it behind an animated advert.

If you get into difficulties, use your onscreen help and any documentation that comes with the CD. Usually there is a ReadMe file at the very least. Read this and, if it is useful, print it before you start the installation itself. Make sure you are not under any time pressure and that you are not going to be interrupted. You will need to concentrate on the job at hand. Otherwise, it will help to have any details you might have gathered about your Internet service provider, including the names of your mail and news servers. But you can always put those in later.

Start by restarting the computer. Don't open any other programs before going straight to the Installer. The CD may start itself, or you may have to find it in My Computer. Mac users, double-click on the CD's desktop icon.

As soon as you start, the installer will start asking you questions. You won't always know the answers – no one does – but it will be clear what the program wants you to answer. The button it wants you to click, whether 'Yes' or 'No', will be highlighted with a darker border. In this way, you agree to a huge licence agreement (basically, you get the program for nothing but can't rewrite or sell it) and let the program load its files on to the disk. If you have plenty of space on your hard disk, and a new machine will have, agree to a 'full' or 'typical' installation. 'Custom' or 'basic' installations are faster and more economical, but you probably won't know what you can safely leave off.

Let the installer choose where it wants to put the program. Unfortunately, when it asks if you want to make the program your 'default', a careful answer is required. Making this browser your 'default', meaning basic starting point, will affect any others you already have. Don't say Yes unless that's what you want.

Then, when it asks if you want to use old settings for things like Favorites/Bookmarks, History and Email, you will have to think. If you are making it your default, and you say no, you risk wiping your old settings for these things without supplying any new ones. Better to say yes if you already have those settings on the machine.

Now, do you want to make the start page of Microsoft/ Netscape/your ISP/your supermarket into your home page? No, because you don't want to go there every time you open the browser, especially if your browser is set to dial up when you open it. You want a blank home page: the browser won't dial up to look at nothing.

Now it wants to know what you want in the way of search facilities. It wants to connect you to Microsoft or Netscape's own search page. Well, it won't do any harm but later you can change it for something better.

After all that, it is finally time to install. Click the Install button that comes up, or click Yes, and a kind of horizontal thermometer bar on screen will show you what's happening. And finally that goes and a browser icon or two will appear on your screen.

Finished? Not quite. When you start the browser, it will try to gather the extra information it needs: usually your account name, which may be the same as the start of your email address or may be your User ID, and the name of your mail servers. All this has been provided by your ISP.

Finally, you get to connect. A panel pops up to show you what's happening: it always has a disconnect button, too, and is one of the ways of ending the connection when you've finished. It will report your speed. Don't be surprised if your 56k modem gets you connected at about 44k. That's how it is.

Your browser suddenly comes to life: words, followed by graphics and pictures. You are at some sort of 'portal' site run by your ISP or browser maker: usually the 'home page' you have rejected. Now you can see why: it's crowded, noisy and crammed with attention-seeking ads. You can register if you like: this will usually 'personalise' your page, meaning you get British headlines and weather rather than American. But you may never see the need to come back to this page again. You have a working browser, and the web is at your feet.

Through a browser darkly

As I said before, a browser does two basic jobs. It connects you to pages and files, whether out there in the Internet or on your own hard disk, and it displays them on screen. But browsers are cosmetically different, even when they are from the same stable. Internet Explorer and Internet Explorer for Mac, for instance, are wildly at odds.

But the fundamentals are identical. First, windows. When you want to look at something, you open a window. If you want that window to show something else, you let the browser find that and display it instead. But you can always open another window, and have your new page displayed there instead. Go to the File menu and select 'New . . .' followed by 'Window' or 'New navigator' in Netscape.

If you have set a blank home page these windows will be blank when you first open them: white in Explorer and grey in Netscape, although you can change that. They are like any other screen window: you can resize or move and scroll over the contents with the scroll bar at the right-hand edge of the screen. That appears only when there is some content to scroll over. Remember, the average web page is much deeper than your little screen window: you must scroll to see it all. Sometimes they are wider too. The presence of the scroll bar indicates that you aren't seeing it all.

Below the viewing area is a grey bar containing various items of information. It says whether you are online or offline. And another thermometer bar grows across the page to tell you how close you are to receiving all the information needed for the page to be finished. Sometimes it flashes once and the page is there. Other times it stops altogether before anything has appeared.

Another icon (a closed padlock) tells you when you are connected to a 'secure' site which encrypts your details – your credit-card number, for instance – as it transfers them. Internet Explorer tells you here what 'security zone' you have created for yourself in the Preferences or Options, which is where such adjustments are made. Most people opt for 'Internet zone': not as secure as it should be, but if you turn your browser into Fort Knox nobody wants to let you into their site.

That's about as far as the similarities of layout between the various browsers can be relied upon. But there are always some common functional controls and facilities, even if they work slightly differently in each case.

The right address

Perhaps even more important than the display window is the Address or Location box. Before the browser can display anything, it has to get it, and the address box tells it what to get. It's a long horizontal white bar, into which you write the web addresses of the sites or pages you want to find. This, at least, is getting easier. Web addresses used to look like this: 'http://www.exxon.com', and you used to have to write it all. Now you can omit the 'http://' because the browser assumes you want a web page. And, if you are dealing with a big American or International company, you can leave out the '.com', too, because it assumes that is what you want. Type in just Exxon and Internet Explorer will take you to the home page of Exxon-Mobil Inc.

Most of the time, though, you have to type in the whole thing. First there's the host and domain name, which may start with 'www' but doesn't have to. Then there's a slash, and then a series of other instructions separated by slash marks until eventually you arrive at the name of the individual file or page you want. If you want to go straight there, you have to get it exactly right. The slightest mistake will halt you in your tracks. Note: if you have put in a space, you won't get a result. No web addresses contain spaces. And in the 'path' section, after the first forward slash, capitals may mean capitals. If you think you have typed it right, however, try chipping bits off the address, slash mark by slash mark, until you get through to something in the same site: there may be a directory or search tool you can use once you are there.

Typing these long and tedious web addresses and file

paths is very tricky. So the people who build browsers have done what they can to make them work as far as possible without any complex typing. They use navigation buttons, and they use various stored lists of previously collected Internet addresses.

Web beginners often open a browser window and then, expecting it to behave like a car, start clicking the 'Forward' button. Nothing happens. In fact the browser is more like one of those old slide projectors that take a set of slides in a straight holder. The person holding the remote control has forward and back buttons, too, but can't go forward or back until he's loaded the first slide. After that, he can go back. Once he's shown two or more, he can go back or forward. That's how the browser's back and forward buttons work.

But once a lot of pages (or slides) have been seen, the browser offers the opportunity to go to any one among them. They are held in the Go menu or 'Go to' submenu in Views. Slide your mouse cursor up and down and pick the one you want to see: it will be reloaded. That list of pages becomes the basis of your History list, accessible through a button or a menu item. In Internet Explorer, this list grows and grows until it reaches a maximum that you specify, and then the older items drop off. In Netscape it is less well handled. In some versions it is wiped when you close the program, which is useless.

Going back to our slide-projector analogy: imagine that the person working the projector put some of the slides on one side so that he could go back to them time and time again. In a browser, that's the basis of a Bookmarks or Favorites list (note the US spelling). Your bookmarks are very useful. If you see a promising page, you can transfer it to your bookmarks list in seconds: go to the Bookmarks/Favorites menu and click on 'Add to Bookmarks' or 'Add to Favorites'. Even if you just see a promising web address in a document, without even going to the page, you can transfer it to your bookmarks, usually by holding your mouse button down or right-clicking until a little menu comes up.

You can edit your bookmarks and send them to your friends by email, because they are very small files, being only the addresses of the pages and not the pages themselves. You can even store them on 'bookmark sites' on the web so you can access them from wherever they are and even share them with other web users: more on that in the Glossary. All in all, bookmarks are some of my favourite things.

There are still lots of other buttons, but most are self-explanatory. Print does what it says, but you need to ensure that you are printing exactly what you want. Some pages are made up of separate frames, making them behave as if they were several web pages displayed alongside one another. Each browser has a different system for ensuring you get the right bit: study your online help files. Then there's the Home button. If you've selected a blank page, it will either be greyed out or take you to a blank page: if you have left things as they are, it will take you to someone else's idea of a home page. Netscape also has a My Netscape button, which takes you to the Netscape start page or 'portal'. Similarly there's a Search button that will either take you to Netscape's or Microsoft's Search page or take you to a search site you choose for yourself. There are lots more of these 'feature' buttons, but none are crucial: sometimes you can choose whether or not you want them. I have an Images button on my browser so I can turn back on Images if I have turned them off to make browsing quicker. More on that later.

The two powerful controls I haven't mentioned yet are Stop and Reload (or Refresh). Stop is the button you press if you are waiting for a page to appear on your screen and you change your mind. It will also stop the irritating process whereby a page you have stored (or an HTML email, about which more later) that you are trying to view offline tries to dial up because some of its pictures or graphics are missing. Click Stop and the dialling should stop. Unfortunately, it usually starts again: three or four attempts and it usually gets the idea. The problem with Stop is that it doesn't exactly interrupt what's going on. Sometimes it waits for a natural break in the flow of data, by which time you might have decided you want to view the page after all. That's when it will stop it.

Click Reload (in Netscape) or Refresh (in Internet Explorer) to bring in the very latest version of a page, or rebuild a page that has not formed itself properly on your screen. If you select a page and it doesn't come, especially if you get a 'busy' notice instead, click Reload or Refresh and you may get through. Often the page is busy for only a fraction of a second. In web-based Chat (see Glossary) you will need to click Reload/Refresh constantly to see the other half of your conversations.

So those are the main controls of a browser. There is also a row of menus, each of which drops down to reveal numerous options for finding your way around the web and dealing with what you find there. Take some time to find out what each menu does, using the built-in Help for reference: everything on these menus should be explained there. Among other things they

- let you open additional windows
- show you what you are printing, and how
- let you bring up a blank email
- save pages on to your hard disk, as text, text and layout (HTML) or complete (in Internet Explorer only, as Web Archive)
- let you find and display pages you have already saved to disk.

This is also where you go to tell the browser that you are working offline, rather than online, and therefore do not want it to dial up to your ISP. Even then, it doesn't always understand. But those are just a few of the options.

Hypertext and hyperlinks

All those controls relate to the idea of the web as a series of individual pages, to be opened one at a time by using their web addresses. But the essence of the web is not that at all: it is hypertext, the idea of linking chunks of type, pictures and whole pages so that your browser can move from one to another without your ever having to type or select an address.

This is how the web started, when web pages were mostly text with the odd picture. By underlining some of the text, or putting it in a different colour, the pioneers of the web indicated that those words could be clicked on to bring a different document or file on to the screen. That remains the organisational principle of the whole web, although those 'hyperlinks' are no longer so obvious. Sometimes the text in question looks much the same as the paragraphs around it. Sometimes the link is embedded in a perfectly ordinary-looking picture: this is almost invariably the case with so-called 'banner' adverts, which are designed as a graphic at the top, bottom or side of a page. Click on them and they take you to the advertiser's site. You can get software to remove them, but most of us take them as the price we pay for a free Internet. But beware of banner ads designed to look like tick boxes and program buttons, usually asking you a direct question. They are a real nuisance.

Sometimes a large picture or graphic will contain lots of different links: it's called an image map, because the designer might use a map of Europe to hide links to British, French, German and Italian sites.

But sometimes you don't want to leave the page you are looking at just to see what is at the other end of a link. You don't have to: modern browsers place a lot of power in your mouse finger. When you click on a link with your right button (hold the button down on the Mac), a little menu appears that offers you the opportunity to look at the contents of the link in a window of its own. This often makes sense, especially if you are working your way through a list of links on a single page. Many worthwhile web sites are made of little else. Indeed, what is Yahoo!, perhaps the most valuable of all web businesses, other than a list of links? Right-clicking, or holding down your single Mac button, produces other options, too. Try them.

Sometimes, however, you will find that clicking on a link opens a new window without your having anything to do with it. That's because the page designer has written that into the code that makes it work: similar code permits areas of type to scroll, allows you to fill in forms and receive an automated answer and so on. These pop-up windows are nothing to be alarmed about: they do a useful job. But they do not enter your browsing history, your box of slides. You can't navigate backwards and forwards to and from them. You just click them when you have finished and they disappear. Usually. There are programmers who will write their pages so that closing one window immediately opens another. And closing that one opens one more. This is an attention-grabbing tactic that seems calculated to infuriate. If it happens to you, your only escape may be to quit the browser, using the keyboard if necessary: CTRL-ALT-DEL in Windows, Command (Apple)-Q in Mac.

That's an example of JavaScript, a programming language that has transformed the web into the all-action kaleidoscope of sound and light we know today. It is not always apparent that this is progress. To make the modern web work, you will find yourself encountering all manner of new programming techniques, languages and file types. Luckily, these are mostly dealt with automatically, but they can still be a menace. Java is a powerful computer language designed to work on any 'platform' (meaning system). It involves creating little programs, 'applets', and running them in a Java area in your computer. When this happens, you will see the dread words 'Applet loading' at the bottom of your screen. Dread words, because they often herald a crash.

There are many more of these advanced technologies: DirectX, JScript, DHTML, Flash, Real and many more. Some, for instance Real's system for live 'streaming' sound, are indispensable. Others are less so. You will find you probably install a Java 'machine' when you install your browser, but it will need to be updated. Other special programs install themselves as 'plug-ins' or 'helpers' when you inadvertently go to a page containing that type of content. They usually ask you if you wish to proceed: half an hour later, you find you have a Flash player or similar, and at least then you don't need to download it next time you go to a Flash-equipped site. Until Flash is upgraded, of course.

Many of the troubles you will face in your normal wanderings around the Internet will come from plug-ins, Java and other types of Active Content. If you are the paranoid type, you should also know that they have been implicated in security problems. See the Glossary for more on that. On the other hand, they are pretty much essential to the web experience today. You can go into your Preferences or Internet Options and switch all this stuff off. But then you'll be back in 1994, and a lot of sites simply won't let you see what they are about.

Cookies are a lot less problematic than some of these technologies: they don't ask you to download programs that take over your computer. But for some reason they get a worse press. In essence all they are is a simple text file that a site gives you when you visit it the first time and then asks for the next time. It doesn't contain any information you haven't volunteered (or at least, that's the theory) and the site uses it so that it knows you have been there before. Then it can say, 'Hello, John.'

If you haven't touched 'Cookies' in your Preferences or Options, you will probably be asked whether you want to accept cookies at every second or third site you visit. This can become very boring, and most people just agree to 'accept all cookies'. They are listed in Preferences/Options and you can even read what they say, if that will help. Refusing to accept them at all will mean you are refused service at some sites. Read the information in the Glossary and follow some links before you decide what to do. Personally, I am convinced they are (mostly) harmless.

Strip down your browser for speed

Do you want your browser to give you the full range of multimedia effects? Or do you want it just to work quickly? You can't always have both, even if you have a fast computer and a fast Internet connection. If speed is your thing, go into the Preferences/Options area (in the Edit or Tools menus) and make a few adjustments.

Start with that blank home page I mentioned. You may also like to specify a 'text-only' tool bar. It won't make things faster, but it will give you a bigger screen area. (In any case, you can usually clear all the controls out of the way temporarily with a keyboard command: check the Help file.)

When you come to the web Content panel, you can take radical steps. Click the little boxes with ticks in them and those options will be disabled. If you want you can safely cancel pictures, animations, sounds, frames, scripting, plug-ins and 'Allow pages to specify their own fonts and colours'. The result will be a bare-bones experience. It will be faster, except when you find a site that won't work without the modern gadgetry, and then your gains will be lost as you go back to the panel, switch it all back on and try again. But I have an 'Images' button on my browser, so I can leave Images switched off until I need them. In fact, that is quite frequently the case. Modern sites often turn essential information into prettily designed image files rather than leaving them in fast, readable text.

Elsewhere, you can switch Java off, but the same problems will occur. You may want to set a 'High' security zone, but that won't help you move around the web speedily and efficiently. Too many sites will fail your browser's new security tests. You may also want to adjust your cache. This holds pages and components of pages to help them load up more quickly the next time you go to them. A bigger cache stores more material and makes it more likely that your computer can find more of what it needs on its own hard disk. However this potential speed gain is somewhat wasted if you allow the browser to go to the site first to compare what it finds there with what it has in the cache. You have three options for controlling this behaviour. 'Once per session' means that you have to wait while it does this the first time you go to a site during any given browsing session (from opening the browser to quitting it). If you go back to the site, it doesn't bother, which speeds things up. 'Always' means that the browser makes this enquiry every time you ask for that page, no matter how many times you have seen it already. That's the slowest option. Finally, there's 'Never'. This means that the computer looks in its cache for what it wants and uses it. If it's not there, it goes to the site. Either way, it's quicker than all that to-ing and fro-ing, but it might mean you aren't seeing the very latest page. But that's all right as long as you remember to manually update it, using the Reload/Refresh button. I have always used the 'Once per session' system, as is usually recommended. But I am experimenting with 'Never': it's quicker.

Nothing else will make much difference, except perhaps if your ISP recommends that you use its web proxy. This is a server computer that stores popular web sites so you can get them locally rather than scouring the world. Ask your ISP about it. If you are convinced, type its address into the web proxy box and tick 'Use web proxy'.

Searching in seconds
It's one thing having a fast, lean browser. It's quite another being able to use it to find anything. The biggest complaint among new users of the Internet is that they can't find anything. Investigate further and what they

usually mean is that they find too much. This is hardly surprising. There are at least 1,000 million web pages out there: type 'football' or 'gardening' into a search box and it shouldn't shock you if you get 100,000 'hits'.

Searching, and research generally, is a fascinating topic. If you are interested, see the Glossary and follow some of the links. Try Search Engine Watch (**www.searchenginewatch. com**) or Research Buzz (**www.researchbuzz**). Both have email newsletters full of interesting hints and information.

But here's a quick, three-step guide to effective finding, as opposed to ineffective searching. I should start by saying that the Internet is not always the best place to look for things. If you know the answer is in a dictionary or an encyclopedia on your shelf, why bother with something as frustrating as the Internet?

First, don't 'search' unless you have to. There are a lot of documents out there, and you don't know where to start. The most important thing in Internet research is to avoid getting swamped and demoralised by too much irrelevant information. If someone has recommended you an Internet address, or you've written down something you saw in an advertisement or an article, use that instead. If you can guess the likely address, try that. The browser will help you out in the case of big public companies, especially if they are American. Type a few variants of the name or its initials into the search box. If they're wrong, you'll find out straightaway. If they're right, you are through to where you want to be. And if there's a specific tool that just does the job you want done, go there. For instance, if you want news headlines from around the world, you would do much better going to Moreover (**www.moreover.com**) or The Paperboy (**www. thepaperboy.com**) than asking search engines for 'world news headlines'.

Secondly, consider using a directory next, rather than a search engine. A directory is a human-assembled or human-edited list of sites, arranged into a hierarchy of categories. The best-known one is **Yahoo!**, but there are lots of others, including **LookSmart, Lycos, Open Directory** and **About.com,** which is not so much a directory as a collection of favourite articles. Directories are best when you don't quite know what you want. You want to know a range of possible sources for stuff about gardening, or the Canadian Pacific railway, or the weather in Washington, DC. But you don't have a specific query. You want to look at the price-comparison sites in Britain, but you don't know any of their names. All these work better in a directory. You navigate a directory by working down through the categories, from a few major headings to the actual sites at the end of the process. Clicking on Business leads you to Publishing, which leads to Magazines, which leads to Consumer, which leads to *Mountain Biking.* Alternatively, the directories have a search box, but it searches only the subject headings and site names, not the wording of individual web pages. So you can put in 'hobby magazines' and then search again in the list of possibles that it brings up. But you'd be surprised. These directories are very broad, but not particularly deep. Sometimes your query will lead you to only a handful of sites.

Thirdly, use search engines when you want something specific. What is Hugh Grant's middle name? Is moss edible? What does the Lord Chancellor earn? Search engines work by taking the words you type into the search box and trying to find out whether they match words in the sites that their computers have analysed. There is no human element in the searching, only in designing the clever software that sorts the results into some sort of useful order.

The secret is to try to create the narrowest search possible, so that your first attempt produces only a handful of responses, or 'hits'. In order to keep the number of hits down, you need to put lots of words into that search box, but almost all the search engines will look first for sites that have all of them before listing those that have only a few of them. So, if you are a worried gardener and you type 'moss' into **www.google.com**, which now claims to know about more than 1,000 million web pages, you won't be surprised to learn that it finds 556,000 pages using the term. But few of them refer to the well-known lawn hazard.

Type in 'moss garden lawn treatment', however, and the picture changes. Now you get 1,255, and most of them are about gardening. Add another couple of words and you'd get a narrower result still.

That's one basic technique: starting narrow and then, if necessary, working outwards. Another is to make use of four simple devices: + (the plus sign); - (the minus sign); * (an asterisk) and ' ' (open and close quotes). These symbols are recognised by most of the search engines, though not all. Work out your search on paper first. Think about the document you want to find: what word or words must it contain? Put a + before each of these. What words should it not contain? Put a - before those. Are there any phrases that must appear exactly? Put those in quotes: 'Hugh Grant' or 'middle name'. Do you want to find several variants on the same word? Use * like this: garden* will bring in garden, gardens, gardener and gardening.

Finally, you would do well to learn to use one search engine really well. All have extensive help files that you can download. I recommend Google because of the clever way it orders sites: it places those that lots of other sites link to, and are thus recommended, at the top. But you can't do a comprehensive search from just one search engine. Although they are vast, they don't actually cross over one another's territory very much. There is a lot more on searching in the Glossary, including how to use 'meta-search', which means searching lots of search sites at the same time.

Bear in mind that even within the web there are lots of sites that cannot be found through search engines. Sites that require you to register and use a password, and sites that store their information in particular types of file – notably

Acrobat .pdf files – cannot be indexed by computerised search tools. If they haven't been indexed, you won't be able to find them from a search engine. Some of these so-called 'hidden web' sites can be found through a directory called The Invisible Web (**www.invisibleweb.com**).

Once you know how to move from link to link and how to search, you have the essential tools to go anywhere on the web and find the things you like. Other useful skills, like downloading files and sending and receiving messages, will come in the next chapter.

Of all Internet activities, shopping is perhaps the most overhyped. If you are a person who really enjoys shopping, you probably won't get a kick out of sitting at your screen clicking on things that appear slowly. Several highly rated and technologically brilliant web stores have failed, or seem likely to fail, because their founders seem not to have appreciated that shoppers are not very interested in buying clothes they can't touch or health products and food that they can't smell. While we wait for the arrival of the web equivalent of 'smellyvision' – and work is already advanced – we might do better to consider when Internet shopping is a good idea.

It works best when you know exactly what you want, mainly because you have seen it in someone's normal bricks-and-mortar shop. Then you can buy it on the Internet if it is cheaper. Things that are often cheaper include books, CDs, software and computer equipment. But you must take into account the cost of post and packaging, which is not always as prominent on the shopping site as the low price. Amazon, for instance, provides a fast and efficient way to buy books, if you know exactly what you want. But its delivery charges are neither easy to find nor particularly appealing, especially if you want only one book.

So always check the cost of delivery before committing yourself. Many sites offer free delivery on orders over a certain price or if you are prepared to wait three to five days. The great thing that the Internet makes possible is automated price-comparison shopping. A site like Checkaprice (**www.checkaprice.co.uk**) makes it possible to type in the name and model number (where appropriate) of a product and then quickly be shown a list of suppliers in order of price. Some of these sites also include delivery charges and details of stock availability. Then you click a link to the shop itself and complete the transaction. If you like buying things, but don't much enjoy shopping, this sort of site has a lot to recommend it.

Once you arrive at the online shop in question, you will be guided through the process. Watch for an icon of a closed padlock in the bottom of your screen. That indicates that you have entered a 'secure' area, where it should be safe to type in your credit-card details because they cannot be intercepted in transit. Remember that even an unsecured link is as safe as a lot of the practices that go on with credit-card slips in dark restaurants. Using a credit card rather than a debit card may give you better protection in the event of problems, depending on which credit-card company you use.

Because this is a tedious process, involving passwords and 'security words' (your mother's maiden name is a popular choice), some shops ask you to establish an account. The next time you come to shop, the process should be much quicker.

Obviously, you need to have confidence in your supplier. At the very least, look around the site to ensure it has a physical base somewhere, so that you can chase it up if things go wrong. Reports suggest that the promise of Internet shopping often falls down at the 'fulfilment' and delivery stage. I use it often, but then I don't like shopping. Recently I bought a printer by using a specialist comparison site, Computer Prices UK (**www.computerprices.co.uk**) and simply selecting the cheapest online store from the list. The process took about 15 minutes, I spoke to no one and I saved 20 per cent on the price of the same item at my local out-of-town computer warehouse. I opted for free delivery, expected it to take five days, but tracked it on the delivery company's website and took delivery in only two working days.

Perfect service: but there was a hole the size of my fist in the packaging. Luckily, whatever made the hole (a fork-lift?) did no damage to the equipment. But that would seem to sum up the Internet shopping experience: excellent when it works, but if it goes wrong you'd rather you hadn't bothered.

4 Leaving the Web

The web can be very impressive, but there is more to the Internet than pretty pages. Indeed, many old-timers take the view that the web is hardly the Internet at all. What interests them, and others who look beyond the glittering billboards of the web, are the older parts of the network where users actually take part.

The chief among these is email. Email may be the most underrated aspect of the whole online world. It doesn't always look like much, but it has a capacity for shaping itself to its users' needs and then hooking them. After all, whoever heard of anyone pacing the streets of a foreign town trying to find somewhere where they can look at a web page? But email users pretty soon come to need their daily shot.

And email need not contain only brief memos about work or from family. That's how we have tended to use it, once again because we have been afraid of spending 'unnecessary' time on line. But a single burst of email, collected in seconds, can contain long letters, newsletters, raging discussions and anything that can be put into digital form: maps, photographs, plans, sounds and even video clips. And if you want, you can even dress email up so it looks like a web page.

And all that stuff can be sent anywhere, instantaneously and effectively for nothing. It can be picked up by anyone on their own computer or one they've borrowed. It doesn't go astray like a fax: it sits there until they pick it up. You can send it while your friends sleep so they get it when they wake up. It can keep them informed of a vital project, or give them a hearty laugh or a wry smile.

And if you're one of those people who send photocopied letters about their families around the world at Christmas, or you've been cajoled into producing a newsletter for your fellow hobbyists, you can send as many copies as you like with a single click. Now you're an email publisher.

Email can be as formal as a business letter or as intimate and cryptic as pencil marks on a Post-it note. You can stick to the facts, or you can go off into flights of fancy. But beware: email is not quite as private as a letter. A couple of clicks of the mouse, and your amusing remarks about the head of your International division will have been copied and pasted to a few hundred more colleagues around the world. People shouldn't, but they do. A marvellous tool, then, but with a few quirks of its own.

How email works

When you send an email, the message you type in is broken up into short 'packets' of information. Each one knows where it's going and where it's from. But they travel separately, reassembling themselves at the far end. If any don't get through, a message comes back asking for them to be sent again. And all this happens instantaneously.

All that packaging is done by your Internet connection software, TCP/IP. Forget about it. You will have much more to do with your own email program, properly known as an email 'client'. This is where you write your message, then fill in the email address, like this: **johnsmith@ smallprovider.co.uk**. Then you click Send, and off it goes to your Internet service provider and from there to the eventual recipient. That's half the job. The other half requires the program to ask your ISP whether there is anything waiting for you in its mailbox. If there is, it asks for it to be sent to your computer. And then it appears in your inbox. Pretty simple, on the face of it.

Email clients

Mail programs have grown so that they now have all sorts of other facilities: the most essential is an address book, but they also have a filing system for all the mail that is flooding in. Some also have a built-in diary and calendar. If you are interested in taking up email publishing, you will need something more complex to help you manage your subscribers. If you want to find email clients, type in those words in the search box in something like www.tucows.com or www.download.com and you will get a glimpse of the possibilities.

But the rest of us find we can manage perfectly well with the email programs that come with our browsers: Outlook Express, if you are using Internet Explorer, and Messenger, if you are using Netscape. Some ISPs recommend a venerable program called Eudora. All are free, or available in free versions. All do effectively the same thing, but they have their quirks. Be very wary if you change from one to another or if you upgrade. Losing a lot of old web pages or your bookmarks or your web preferences is a nuisance, but losing your entire email filing cabinet and address book is more like a disaster, and it can easily happen. The latest version of Outlook Express for the Mac, for instance, consolidates all your email files into one huge database document, and then stores it in the application folder, where you would least expect it to be. So copy your existing program before you install anything new.

Let's take a look at the basics of a typical Email program, Outlook Express 5 for Windows. They all have their strengths and weaknesses. Outlook Express has a complex system for handling multiple email accounts, which is a boon to people in Britain who are constantly juggling ISPs to get a good deal. It also has built-in support for Hotmail (see Glossary). To launch it, you use a 'short-cut' icon: you should make sure you have one, either on your desktop, or in your taskbar. If not, make one by finding the program itself, somewhere in the bowels of your C drive (that's your hard drive), and clicking on your right mouse button. 'Create Shortcut', it says: now click and hold with your left button and drag the shortcut to your desktop. If it ends up saying something like 'Shortcut to msimn.exe', rename it 'Outlook Express'. In the Mac, find the program, make an alias and stick it on the desktop or in the Apple menu.

When the program window opens, it brings with it the pop-up for the Dial-up Connection. You can Connect, or Work Offline. Let's work offline. To set how the program behaves when you open it, go to Options in the Tools menu and make sure the 'Send and receive messages at startup' box is not ticked. There are a whole pile of possible adjustments here, not only for email but also for reading newsgroups. Leave them as they are for the time being: make changes as you learn more.

So, we've stopped it dialling up, and we can close the Dial-up box and see the main program window again. It opens to the Inbox, which has two horizontal panels. In the top are listed the headings and senders of all the incoming messages. At the bottom, the top message in that list has been blown up so you can read it. If you double click on the highlighting, it opens in a window of its own, and this window has a couple of arrows in the button bar allowing you to skip through your mail, one message at a time as well as letting you see your address book, forward the message or reply.

In the same way we avoided typing any web addresses, we avoid typing email addresses. Clicking 'Reply' produces a blank space to type in, with the sender's name now moved to the 'To:' panel. The subject of their original (let's say it was 'Books') now becomes 'Re: Books'. Type in your reply, click Send, and you've done your duty: no wonder people manage to reply to their own emails (and indeed, a prompt reply is expected). Note that in some programs, depending on how you have set them up, the entire content of the incoming message will have been copied into your reply, usually in a different colour and marked off by signs like this: >>>>>. Leave the bits that are necessary to remind the person what their letter was about. This really helps busy people.

If you were to click the Reply All button, you would send your reply to all the recipients of the original message. If you are just one in a cast of thousands receiving that particular circular, this would not be a good idea. If you click Forward, on the other hand (nothing to do with the Forward button on your browser) the entire message will be copied and sent on to anyone whose address you type into the 'To:' box. Not that you have to type, usually. You just go to the 'To:' icon next to the address box and click your mouse button. An address book will appear, at which point you can decide whom you'd like to receive the message.

That box also offers the opportunity to send copies of your reply to other people. You can send either CC copies, meaning 'carbon copies', or you can send what are called 'Bcc' or 'blind carbon copies'. The difference is that those receiving carbon copies know who else got a copy; those receiving blind carbon copies aren't told. If you don't want people to know who sent the message, put yourself in the 'To:' box, and all your real recipients in the 'Bcc' category.

This is a useful, much abused facility. Bulk emailers, commonly known as spammers, like to send everyone in the world a copy of their latest 'GET RICH QUICK EARN $$$$$' leaflet. But they don't want people to know who sent the message or rival spammers to get hold of their mailing lists. So blind carbon copies are the order of the day.

OK, now we've sent a reply, or multiple replies, and we've forwarded a message. But what about a new message? Easy. In the main Inbox button bar, there's a 'New Mail' button. If your program hasn't got that, go to the File menu and put your pointer over New. You can bring up an outgoing-mail message in exactly the same

way in Internet Explorer or Netscape. You must choose
whether you want a mail message or a news message.

After all that, writing and sending a new email message
(usually just called an email) is simple. Your 'From:'
details are already filled in, although you might have to
change them if you have multiple email accounts. We'll
come to that.

If you have the recipient in your address book already,
you don't have to type that. You may even find it starts to
fill itself in as you type. That's Microsoft's famous 'auto-
correct' at work: it doesn't read your mind, but finds the
existing address somewhere in the mail folder and works
from that. Not so spooky, especially if you switch it off in
Options.

Incidentally, you don't have to type email addresses into
your onscreen Address Book. If you get a message from
someone and think you are going to contact them again,
ask the email program to transfer their address to the
address book. It's a menu entry under Tools: 'Add to
Address Book' or 'Add Sender to Address Book'. If you
are using Outlook Express for Windows, go into Tools/
Options/Send and you'll find you can get it to automatically put every address you reply to into your address
book. That might be overdoing it.

If you haven't got the correct address in your address
book, but you are reading it from something on screen,
you may be able to drag and drop it into the slot by highlighting it, holding down your mouse button and moving
it. Failing all that, you'll have to type it after all. Make
sure you get it right: the Internet has no equivalent of the
friendly local postman, sorting out misaddressed letters
and getting them to their rightful homes.

You will want to give your message a subject. Preferably a meaningful one, too. 'Hello there' might make sense
now, but in three months' time, when the recipient is
sorting through their accumulated mail hoping to find
your recommendations for dealing with uncontrolled moss

in the garden, they would really rather be looking for 'moss control – the answer'.

The email itself can be as letter-like as you want. You can write 'Dear Sir' if you think it's appropriate, or you can put 'Hi', or 'Hello', or nothing at all. Similarly with the sign-off. 'Yours sincerely'? 'Best wishes'? 'Ciao, baby'? It's up to you, but the key principle is 'appropriateness'. Are you writing to your bank manager or your eleven-year-old niece? Or someone in Australia, who may be man, woman, young or old, friendly or fierce?

There is no fixed approach to this kind of thing, not least because email exchanges come in so many different shapes. You may swap ten messages in a day in the case of a hot project or some new enthusiasm. Then the wires may go dead for a week. Sometimes you are left wondering whether you have offended the other party, but usually you haven't. They just had to do something in the real world, and then the moment for the perfect reply had passed. The correspondence will start again, or it won't.

Some people end their email with a 'signature'. This is a block of stored text that supplies extra information, perhaps your normal postal address and telephone number if you are happy to have those things known. Some people add an inspirational or amusing quote: 'There are two classes of people: those who divide people into two classes and those who don't'. Others make a little picture out of type. If you feel inclined to follow suit, don't overdo it. Five lines of signature is an absolute maximum.

In the same vein, think before you start dressing up your email. Originally, email was plain text. It didn't take up much room in storage or transit and moved quickly. Then people discovered HTML email: in other words, they found that you could dress email up so it looks exactly like a web page. Most email programs will do either. So you may be able to write your message in HTML, incorporating bold and italic type, different paragraphing styles, graphics and even photographs. The HTML option (or 'Rich Text', which is much the same) is accessible from the Format menu. Select it, and a tool bar appears, offering fonts, type sizes and everything you'd expect in a basic word processor. All very pretty.

But will everyone you send it to be able to read it? And, even if they are, will they want to? Or would they prefer just the real stuff and less of the trimmings? I know my answer. HTML email is a particular menace to those of us who set up our email programs so they dial up, collect our messages and then disconnect. If one of those messages is in HTML, it will sit in your mailbox until the first time you open it. Then, because it is missing its photographs and graphics, it will immediately attempt to dial up to your ISP to get them. This is an experience most of us find we can live without, especially since the HTML mail files are anything up to 10 times the size of a comparable plain-text email.

If you really want to send photographs and graphics to people, the way to do it is by adding an 'attachment'. Somewhere on the button bar of your new message window will be a button that says 'Attachment' or 'Attach'. It may have a picture of a paperclip alongside it. Click it, and various dialogue boxes will appear so that you can specify the type of attachment you want to send and where it is to be found. It has to be encoded to travel over the wires, but that process is effectively automatic. If you are trying to send from Windows to Mac, or even somewhere more peculiar, it may not work, in which case you'll have to look more closely at the encoding options. Mac to Windows works fine as long as you specify 'Apple Double' encoding.

That's the basics of receiving and sending email. The other huge part of an email program involves storing the material that comes in. You can move it into different folders according to topic, or you can have the program do it automatically. In this way, you can set up filters for junk email, the famous 'spam'. See Glossary for more on that.

In order to make your email program work, of course, you must have it set up properly. When you set up an Internet connection using a CD from an ISP or by using your computer's built-in assistance, your email account will normally be set up at the same time. If it doesn't work, it's usually because you typed the password or username slightly inaccurately and your computer has recorded it like that. You will have to go through the process again. If you add extra accounts, and many people do, you are multiplying your problems.

That process is simple enough. In Internet Explorer, go to Tools, then find New Account Signup and do what it says. Once you have your accounts, all the details are kept under Accounts in that same menu. But they are, as always with Windows, vastly overcomplex. By all means have a look round the cluster of control panels that emerges, but write down all the existing settings before you change anything. Netscape, meanwhile, really doesn't like multiple email accounts.

If you sign up to a new ISP and it destroys all your old account settings, then that ISP must help you sort things out. If you want to tackle your own problems, they are most likely to come in four areas: your user ID or Login; your password; your outgoing mail-server name and your incoming mail-server name. Your user ID and password must be exactly as agreed with your provider. Sometimes the user ID is exactly the same as the beginning of your email address, the bit before the @ sign.

But often it is a string of meaningless numbers and letters that you use to gain access to your mail account: you will have a different, more memorable email name. Either way, it must be typed in correctly: your computer will remember it, and your password. Your password can always be changed: your ISP will usually have a place on its website where that can be done. Some providers don't allow you to change your user ID after first signing up.

Then there are the two mail 'server' names. The servers

are the computers at your ISP that hold your mail before sending it on or waiting for you to collect it. Mail coming to you from the outside world uses a system called POP3. The 'receiving' server's name is likely to begin with 'pop', 'pop3' or 'popmail', followed by your provider's domain name. Thus your incoming mail server might be called: pop. smallprovider.co.uk. Outgoing or 'sending' mail goes by a system called SMTP. Outgoing mail server names start 'smtp' or 'mail' or 'mailhost', like this: smtp.smallprovider. co.uk.

Don't get them the wrong way round, or you will get nowhere. Incidentally, you don't have to be on your own computer to pick up your POP3 mail. You can get it through a web-based mail-forwarding site, but only if you know the name of your POP3 server. So those odd addresses can come in useful.

Finally, make sure you have the right number for the ISP in the Dial-up settings (or Remote Access if you're a Mac user). I once spent three days trying to get through to a provider using the number given on its website: the number was out of date, but the website hadn't been changed.

None of this stuff is particularly enjoyable to deal with. If you don't make headway by checking these obvious things, you'd do better to get someone else to help you out, particularly since, if you get it wrong, it can knock out all your communications until you put things right. Remember to keep backups of your precious email folders and address book when you are messing about in this area.

It's worth noting that you can set up your email so that a call to one provider will collect email addressed to you at any of the others. But it doesn't work the other way round: to send email from a particular provider, you must actually dial that provider. In other words, to send mail using a johnsmith@smallprovider.co.uk address, John Smith must dial up to the smallprovider computers. But if he dials up to his **johnsmith@largeprovider.com** address, he can also collect mail from his **johnsmith@smallprovider. co.uk** box at the same time.

More important than all these technicalities is the way you use email. Typing away late at night can seem very intimate, and all manner of relationships have been known to develop. But in practice most people see email as existing in a grey area between private letter and public print. It is effortless to highlight a paragraph from one email and copy it across into another. It might not be good manners to share your private thoughts with lots of strangers, but it happens.

What's more, email is almost always kept by the recipients. Finding what you said about something three years ago is as easy as clicking on the Find button or unearthing it in the Edit menu. Think twice about what you are writing. Would you like everybody to hear you saying this? Will you stand by it tomorrow, next week, next year? Could it ever be used against you? Increasingly, emails to and from public organisations and companies are playing a part in legal actions. No one is suggesting you shouldn't have frank exchanges via email but remember, it's not necessarily between the two of you. And that's even before we start asking whether the government is prying . . .

Mailing lists and email discussions

All these questions come to the fore when we talk about Mailing Lists, sometimes called email clubs, which are one of the great secrets of the Internet. Every couple of days, free of charge, you can have email magazines, newsletters or discussions dropped into your email box. They can be fascinating, full of detailed hints and tips that you won't find elsewhere, or buzzing with arguments about subjects so obscure that you never thought you'd find another person who knew about them. And that's the point: the Internet is so huge, and has so many contributors, that you can usually find enough people to discuss anything.

The main types of Mailing List are these. A simple, 'unmoderated' discussion list has no one controlling the contributions. A short comment on something arrives in your mailbox and that of everyone else who has subscribed to it. You reply, and your reply too is automatically sent to everyone on the list. In busy times, you receive several individual contributions a day.

In a variant of this, the contributions are distributed in digest form, perhaps weekly or even more frequently. This is much more manageable: one large file a week that you can 'scroll' your way down until you find something interesting. Such a digest may not be 'moderated', but it usually is. A 'moderated' discussion list will have rules, enforced by the moderator. These are often no more than an occasional clampdown on boring topics and commercial self-interest among participants. Otherwise, the arguments and the language can be decidedly untrammelled. If that doesn't worry you, these lists can be great.

But there are also a large number of 'closed' mailing lists, which are effectively email newsletters, written or edited by their creator or by a company or organisation. When you install new software, you are often invited to join such a list, and many websites use them as a more immediate, more active form of publishing. But there are lots of lists that are produced by enthusiasts alone and distributed to their friends.

To find a list and subscribe, try going to a site like **www.liszt.com**, which styles itself the Mailing List Directory. There you will find a Yahoo!-style directory and a search box. Type in 'garden', say, and about sixty lists are suggested. Of these, some are entirely inappropriate ('Garden City Macintosh Users') but a few look interesting. Click on 'Greenthumb', described as 'Discussion of Gardens, Lawns and Related issues', and you go to a page that, unfortunately, doesn't tell you much about the list, but tells you what you have to do to get information. These lists are automated: you send an email with the appropriate wording in the message field and you can get information, sign up, sign off and so on.

In this case, all it wants is 'info greenthumb', but be sure to put it in the message body, not the subject heading, or it will come bouncing back. The info file comes back almost immediately. The list is sponsored by a seed company, which promises to drop in from time to time, but it insists that the list is the work of readers and gardeners. Worth a try?

Now you have to send another message, with 'subscribe greenthumb' in the text panel. And, when that is received, you have to send another, with an authorisation code just to prove that you have actually asked for the list. Mailing-list operators go to great lengths to ensure that people actually want their products: if you ever receive a mailing list you haven't asked for, that's spam. But after all that you are sub-scribed: a welcome message drops into your email box. Now all you need are the actual contributions.

Another link on the Liszt page lends to some general advice about lists. The important one is this: if you are not careful, any email you send will go to the entire list. List people are perfectly friendly, but they don't like it when their mailing consists of little but people trying to 'un-subscribe'. All that type of thing should go to the list's administrative address. But all that is made clear on the initial email you receive when you sign up. Keep it safe, for if and when you want to unsubscribe.

It should be pretty clear whether you have joined a 'free-for-all' discussion or something more genteel. But keep your head down for a bit, 'listen' to what goes on, and then chip in if you have something useful to say. No one minds 'lurkers', people who read but don't contribute. But list members are less keen on people who feel a compulsion to contribute when they have nothing useful to say.

Liszt is wide-ranging, but doesn't give a lot of informa-tion up front. For a different approach, try **www.egroups. com**. But you might want to click on the Family Filter unless you're broad-minded. There are a lot of groups here with only one thing on their minds: and it's not gardening.

But eGroups very helpfully tells you how many members each group has, and gives you a lengthy statement by its proprietor. It also shows how many messages the group generated in recent months. Some of these little communities are tiny and almost inactive, but, when the Internet itself is so vast, that can be rather nice. All in all, mailing lists can be fun, and they can give you valuable information and fresh gossip. And no trees are chopped down to bring them to you.

Newsgroups: read all about it

Rarely has anything laboured under such a misleading name as the Internet's huge collection of 'newsgroups'. Also known as 'Usenet', meaning 'Users' Network', these discussion groups specialise in gossip, invective, abuse and wild speculation. Anything but news, in most cases. While the mailing lists benefit from the fact that people try to think a little before they start tapping away, the newsgroups thrive on sudden brainwaves and instant reactions. Naturally, they can be great fun, but it must be said that most of the things that give the Internet a bad name are to be found in the newsgroups.

To gain access to them, you will probably use your email program initially. But if you are serious about Usenet you may well want to try a dedicated 'newsreader' program. There are lots, at various prices and with varying degrees of sophistication. Go to one of the big FTP download sites (see Glossary).

Newsgroups work as a continuous rolling discussion on any number of different topics. Each group can have hundreds of simultaneous discussions going on at once, but they don't happen in 'real time'. Instead, something catches your eye so you send in a comment. That is added to the end of that particular message 'thread'. Then someone else sees it and adds another comment, or starts a new thread.

And so on. You can't guarantee that the person you are arguing with is going to write straight back: they may be asleep, because they're on the opposite side of the world.

This collection of messages is originally hosted on a single computer somewhere, but copied to news servers all over the world. Your ISP will have one, perhaps several, of these big computers. There are at least 60,000 newsgroups operating at any time, but no ISP will offer all the groups. They tend to rule out those in foreign languages, and those suspected of harbouring illegal activities. Different ISPs adopt different policies about this.

To start using news, you need to download the list of groups from your ISP. When you were setting up your email accounts you should have been prompted to include a news server. Normally its name will begin with 'news', like this: **news.smallprovider.co.uk**. An icon for it will then appear in your list of accounts, or under the Tools menu. Click or double-click on it and the list will either appear or the program will ask if it should start down-loading the list. Don't be surprised if this takes fifteen minutes or more.

When you get the list, you can use the search box at the top of the window to find subjects you are interested in. Newsgroup names work like this: at the far left come the major topic headings, 'rec' for recreation; 'alt' for alternative; 'soc' for social; 'comp' for computers; 'sci' for science; 'talk' for arguments; and so on. There are also local topic headings: 'uk' is Britain. After that, separated by dots, come smaller and smaller subdivisions: rec.music. beatles.info, for instance, which discusses information about something called the Beatles that involves music in a recreational sense. Many of these newsgroup names make little or no sense.

To see what's going on in the group, you simply double-click on its name in the newsgroup list. The modem dials up, and the headings of the current discussions appear in the top part of the window. As it happens, this particular group is very quiet. Perhaps everyone in the world knows everything they want to know about the Beatles. When I looked, there were six items, with no follow-ups attached. To read one, click on it. We discover details of new radio interviews by Ringo and Paul in the US, and that the man who first promoted them in Italy has died. Info indeed.

What about something more controversial? Gun control, say. Back to the long list, type in 'gun' and see what emerges. What about talk.politics.guns? This time, when I tried, 91 headings came in, and a symbol on the left showed that many of these contained numerous contributions. One said '2nd amendment confusion'. Clicking a little arrow on the 'threading' icon reveals four contributions. Double-clicking opens up 'Chuck's' original in a big window. Now up and down arrows let us jump from 'post' (a newsgroup article) to 'post'. And we can see the American gun-control debate, and Usenet in general, in all their glory: in four short messages, everything from learned debate on the precise meaning of the wording of the Second Amendment in the eyes of those who framed it to paranoid ranting about 'fascist victim-disarmers' who want to take patriotic Americans' guns away. Some newsgroups are 'moderated', just like some lists. They will tend to have 'moderated' in their name.

One other thing to note. The presence of the word 'binaries' in a group name means it exists to disseminate not words but computer files: these are usually pictures, sounds, music or computer programs. This is where the porn, the copyright infringement and the viruses live.

Try a software group, say **alt.binaries.emulators.nintendo** and watch the little box that counts how many headers have been downloaded. It shoots straight to 300 and stops, and then only because the program is set to bring in only 300 at a time. Your email program will normally turn these binary files back into something your computer can use.

Not all the binaries groups are disreputable, by the way. Go to **alt.binaries.pictures.rail** and you'll find some lovely shots of Canadian Pacific locomotives. But look at the stuff that appears either side of it in the newsgroups list. That's the Internet for you.

It is one thing to 'lurk' in Usenet. But sooner or later you will want to contribute. Here many people recommend anonymity, or the sort of pseudo-anonymity that comes from setting yourself up so that a pseudonym appears in the 'author' column of the article list. Your real email address will probably still appear on the message itself. Of course, you can always start an email account using a false name throughout the process: since you're not paying, the free ISP doesn't even need to know your real address or bank details. But rest assured, you can still be tracked down if you do anything illegal.

There are two reasons why anonymity might be useful: you can have a lively and controversial time in the world of Usenet without having any repercussions in your real life; and it might prevent you collecting massive amounts of 'spam'. See the section on spam in the Glossary. Newsgroup users attract spam because 'robot' email-address collectors go there to do their work. You can tinker with your email address to make this less likely to happen, usually by inserting phrases such as REMOVE THIS into the 'From' box of your outgoing mail.

All very clever, but a real nuisance for anyone who might want to contact you. Spam, after all, is just junk mail. It's a mild irritant, although the same can't be said of massive and malicious email attacks. But the cures for ordinary spam are often out of all proportion to the harm it does.

As for anonymity . . . It has its uses, and is a longstanding tradition on the Internet. But I like to think I know who I am talking to, and I am happy for people to know they are talking to me. Anonymous messages in Usenet, especially in the sensible areas – and there are plenty – are the equivalent of anonymous letters to the newspapers, or to the boss. They don't necessarily reflect well on those sending them. But if you really need to make anonymous contributions to email lists or Usenet, perhaps because you're a renegade MI5 agent, you will want to use the services of an anonymous remailer: details in the Glossary, or try **www.anonymizer.com**.

It is true that there are sensible and interesting areas in Usenet, but they are not necessarily best found by trawling through the long list. You would do better to go to a specialist Usenet search tool. For a long time the leader in this field was Deja (**www.dejanews.com**), but it has unfortunately tried to turn itself into a shopping site and diluted its *raison d'être*. The Usenet search tools are still there, but only if you follow a small link at the top of the main page, marked 'Discussions'. Type in 'moss' and you'd be amazed: 'Can I eat Sphagnum moss?' asks PaulO2 in **rec.gardens.edible**. 'If you want to,' replies Henrietta, from Finland. 'It's not toxic, but it's not very edible either.' And on the discussion goes.

Deja, and sites like it, look at Usenet through the web, but in many ways this is preferable. You can do an advanced search, setting date limits and choosing only certain groups. You can go to the top of the thread and follow it, or you can read all the posts in a group on a certain date. It's a very useful tool, and it's a pity Deja has decided to bury it behind a lot of stuff about choosing the right baby carriage. You can also try RemarQ (**www. remarq.com**), but it is lightweight in comparison.

These days I sometimes use Forum One (**www.forumone. com**), which claims to search more than 310,000 web 'forums'. These are web-based discussions. They lack the sheer madness of Usenet, but they can be useful in their own way. My search for 'moss' took me to a site called **gardentown.com**, which has a discussion area called Sage Hall. Unfortunately, the 'moss' question had disappeared. That's the Internet for you.

Remember, when you 'post' to the newsgroups or any other forum, that there is every likelihood that your contribution will be held in a searchable archive for a very long time. If that worries you, then you may want to think some more about anonymity or nicknames. These discussion search sites also allow you to join in the discussions you find without having to go back to your email program, but you must register.

In Usenet, though not necessarily in the web-based forums, you are allowed and indeed encouraged to write direct to participants if that is more appropriate than continuing the public discussion. There's a button at the top of your email program to let you 'Reply to Sender' as opposed to replying to that point in the group or starting a new thread. Obviously, if you search the archives and find a fascinating article about moss, you will need to write to the author because the discussion will be long forgotten.

Plenty of people will give you advice on the 'Netiquette' of posting to newsgroups. Mostly it comes down to being civil with strangers, but you should also avoid trying everyone's patience by asking questions that everyone has asked before. Every newsgroup has an FAQ, a list of Frequently Asked Questions with their answers. It usually lives in the newsgroup, or you can download it from a central source: they can be big files. Details in the Glossary.

Chat

These are all ways in which people around the world can discuss things and exchange stuff. Mailing lists and newsgroups have a built-in delay. They depend on your reading something, writing a response, sending it and then waiting for that response to be published or distributed. If that is too slow for you, you might be interested in what is universally known as Chat.

Chat is not spoken discussion. It's written exchanges where both parties (or all parties, since you can chat in groups) are actually present at the same time. In mailing lists or news, you might think about something overnight before responding. In Chat, you type and then I type, and then someone in New Zealand types, and all our messages appear one below the other on screen, in the order they arrive.

There is a section on this in the Glossary. Briefly, Chat falls into two major categories. The first is web chat, which you can do without any extra software. You do have to register with a webchat operator, who will equip you with a suitable nickname and point you in the direction of any of thousands of chats, all going on at once. Most of the big 'portals' have a webchat element: try Yahoo!. Once you have completed the registration, you have a nickname and can leap into any of the discussions. Your nickname appears on screen as being present in the group, but you don't have to say anything. Sometimes a dozen participants are listed and the chat area is totally silent.

Unfortunately, web chat isn't the real thing. Mostly, you have to reload the page each time you send to see your comment and any other new contributions. This is tedious.

Real Chat always requires extra software on your computer. If you are interested in straightforward, simple exchanges with people you already know or can arrange to 'meet' online, you might be happy with one of the 'instant' message systems. The leader in the field is probably AIM, the AOL/Netscape system. Microsoft has a system, too. In fact there are several, some compatible with each other but mostly not.

AIM sits in a button on your browser. When you are online you can ask it to look to see who else you know (and who uses the software) is also online. Then you can send them a message, which gives them an alert on their screen, and the conversation begins. Good fun, and not threatening. All of these systems allow either 'private' chat of this sort or discussions with other people, singly or in gangs, from among their membership base. If that sort of thing is for you, try ICQ, which is something of a cult.

None of these systems conforms to the traditional

Internet standard for Chat, which is called IRC, Internet Relay Chat. Once again, you need to download special software. But now you are in the wide roaring river of Internet babble rather than in a quiet tributary. It is much more tricky to use than the commercial systems, and the inhabitants speak in cryptic codes and verbal shorthand. But there are masses of them, yabbering away 24 hours a day. Is Chat worth bothering with? I'm with Arnold Bax, who said he'd try anything once, except incest and folk-dancing. Those who consider the Internet a great waste of time will find plenty of ammunition in IRC Chat, which can often make you feel like the barman at someone else's teenage party or school reunion. Socratic dialogue it ain't. But it can be addictive, especially for the young, and that addiction can lead to the development of dangerous situations. If you let your young teenagers go to these parties, be wary of any attempt to transfer those relationships into real life. You can come to only so much harm while you are separated from danger by a million miles of wiring. Whereas if you agree to meet someone at Milton Keynes railway station . . .

What all these parts of the Internet have in common is that they are typed. While it's certainly possible to operate your computer using spoken commands, with the right software, you'd be hard pushed to make a real contribution to any of these discussions by speaking and expecting the computer to turn that into script. They are a written medium, and transcribed speech is not writing. The best single skill you can learn to make you a more efficient and involved Internet user is typing. There are plenty of typing tutorial programs available, many of them free. One of the differences between Mailing Lists and Chat is that the people in Chat can't type quickly enough to make themselves understood. If you learn to type, as opposed to jabbing the keyboard optimistically, you won't have that problem.

Internet telephony and spoken chat

Like any other electrical signal, the sounds from a microphone can be put in digital form. Then they can be broken
up into packets of information and sent whizzing around
the Internet, before being reassembled at the receiver's
computer and turned back into sound. So you can use the
Internet for phone calls and for having spoken chat (a tau-
tology, but a necessary one) with strangers. Unfortunately,
both you and the person at the other end need to be
running exactly the same software. You also need the right
hardware, although most new computers will come with a
microphone and speakers. To 'telephone' that person, you
need their IP number, the fixed Internet address of their
computer. And when you get through your phone call will
face the same problems as our BBC news clip and our
bursts of Internet radio. Constant net congestion will
mean the call is interrupted; and, when you *can* hear each
other, you will be shocked to discover that you both sound
like Donald Duck.

So why do it? One word: money. Internet international
calls cost, well, 0p a minute if you have an unmetered provider. A call to the USA on the telephone will cost 20p a
minute. For this reason, Internet telephony and the associated spoken chat are a growing thing. People are constantly announcing ways in which computer users can
make calls to ordinary telephones without setting the call
up in advance. But do you know anyone who does it? I
don't. It's like buying a Lamborghini and then using it to
tow your caravan. There are better ways to use your time
online.

Games

Does playing games come into that category? It depends on
how much games mean to you. There is a huge amount of
games-related activity on the Internet. Some of it relates to
modern, commercial software. You can download endless
free demos, and even whole programs for a fee; you can find

lots of information on 'cheats' and 'patches' to make your own games work better. You can join special networks to play some games against other people, although normally everyone in the shared game must own the full CD of the program itself. Try Wireplay (**www.wireplay.com**) or Kali (**www.kali.net**). The most famous of these games is Quake, a serious obsession among a lot of people with powerful computers and too much time on their hands.

Otherwise, there are masses of special games that can be played on the web, usually requiring you to download various plug-ins. Then you play against the computer, or against other callers at the site. In this category come gambling sites, where you can sign up to lose real money without actually seeing a real roulette wheel in motion. If you are mad enough, you'll find them quite easily.

And then there are the old text-based games involving dungeons, dragons, witches and warlocks, which unaccountably branded a generation of computer enthusiasts as adolescent fantasists. These are often called MUDs (multi-user dungeons) and feature role-playing in elaborate alternative universes. You're asking the wrong person about these: I couldn't understand Dungeons & Dragons when it was played with dice. Try a Yahoo! search for 'MUD' if you are interested. Usually extra software is involved because you must 'Telnet', meaning operate a mainframe computer from your desktop by remote control.

Like Chat, games have an addictive quality, leading at the very least to hogging of the phone line. One more reason for unmetered access. There is more on games in the Glossary.

FTP

In contrast to games, FTP offers something for everyone. It stands for File Transfer Protocol, which is the method used to send files around the Internet. But these days you don't even have to know that. All it means in practice is that there are huge archives of valuable files, both documents and programs, that are yours to download to your own computer. Sometimes there's a commercial charge, sometimes the material is 'shareware', meaning you pay a fairly modest fee (perhaps just sending the programmer a postcard), and very often you pay nothing at all. The FTP business is handled automatically by your browser, but it is worth remembering that when you see a URL that begins 'ftp://' you are downloading something rather than just looking at it. There are lots of large archives of files, some of them listed in the Glossary.

Even though FTP is incorporated into browsers, it is not necessarily as easy as looking at a web page. Some FTP sites, usually the large commercial ones, have organised their files to suit the web. But, when you click on an FTP link to others, you will find yourself faced with an old-fashioned computer directory familiar to those who started with an Amstrad or an MS-DOS machine, but otherwise baffling. Actually, a lot of library catalogues look like this: a page full of little folders on the left with abbreviated names beside them. Click on any one, and you go down a level in the directory: more folders, more meaningless names.

If you find yourself in this sort of FTP site, look for a folder marked 'PUB'. That's the public stuff. Once you're in there, see if you can find a file (looking like a piece of paper) called 'Index' or 'ReadMe' or 'Directory'. That may tell you what's available. In general, though, you need to know the name of an FTP file before you go looking for it in this way. If you find a link to it on a web page, of course, the job is done for you.

If you have to search FTP archives, however, you are entering more complicated territory, requiring special tools with jokey names such as Archie, Gopher, Veronica and Jughead. Thankfully, most of the world's FTP sites and 'Gopher holes' are transferring their indexes to web pages, meaning they can be searched with the usual search tools.

Anything you download could be carrying a virus. It

makes sense to take precautions, perhaps by downloading it to a special folder and running your antivirus program over it.

Putting something back

So far the emphasis has all been on what you can get from the Internet. But the Internet is not television: it's not a broadcasting device, in which a few send their thoughts and creations to the many. It is a device for communication, and, if you are to get the most from it, you will want to take part. Join things, exchange ideas, send emails and then think about producing a website of your own, or producing your own email newsletter.

Neither is particularly difficult, and there is plenty of help available online and in books. I don't want my grandchildren to ask me what I was doing while the Internet changed from a vibrant global meeting place to a sort of video shopping mall.

The Internet is not as easy to use as perhaps it might be, but that only makes it more rewarding for those who make the effort. However you plan to use the Internet, relax – and enjoy it. I hope the glossary and selected websites that follow help you to understand, and get the most out of, this exciting new medium.

5   Glossary: an A–Z of the Net

A

Abbreviations

The Internet is full of abbreviations, acronyms and initials. Some of these are for technical things with cumbersome names. By using the abbreviation MP3s, for instance, you can discuss and exchange digital music files without knowing what MP3 actually stands for.

But there is also a tradition of using abbreviations for ordinary phrases, particularly in email, newsgroups and chat. Early users of computer networks wanted to be able to type as fast as they could speak, so that they could chat and argue. Although their abbreviations are dying out, you may still come across some of the following:

BTW = By The Way
FAQ = Frequently Asked Questions
FWIW = For What It's Worth
<g> = Grin (meaning 'I'm making a joke')
HTH = Hope This Helps
IMHO = In My Humble Opinion
LOL = Laughing Out Loud
My 0.02¢ = My two cents (my opinion)
ROTFL = Rolling On The Floor Laughing
RTFM = Read The ****ing Manual

A comprehensive and not entirely believable list is maintained at **www.astro.umd.edu/~marshall/abbrev.html**.

Acrobat

A 'portable document format' used to produce documents on computers that can replace paper documents. They are like a photograph of a document, with type and illustrations in place. Acrobat files are found all over the web and have largely replaced printed manuals for software. Their names end in '.pdf' and they must be opened, read and printed using the free Acrobat Reader program. You may already have this, or you can get it on the free cover CD-ROMs that come with computer magazines or by downloading from Adobe, its inventor: **www.adobe.com/acrobat**.

Acronyms

An acronym is a set of initials that can be pronounced as a word: for instance, 'laser' or 'scuba'. The Internet has a few: ASCII (pronounced *asky*); JPEG (*jay-peg*); GIF (*giff* or *jiff*); GUI (*gooey*); MIDI (*middy*); MPEG (*empeg*); and WYSIWYG (*whizzywig*). All are defined in this glossary.

Address

The Internet is made up of millions of computers and billions of files containing information, including words, pictures, video and sounds. Each computer and each file made available on the net has its own 'address' to indicate where it can be found. These addresses may look like a random string of letters, numbers and punctuation marks, but they contain valuable information. And they can be read, just like the address on an envelope.

Email addresses are easily identified because they contain an @ symbol. Take, for example, **johnsmith@smallprovider. com**. Everything before the @ is the 'username' of an individual email customer. The bit after the @ is the name of the organisation providing the email service. An organisation can dish out as many usernames as it likes, but every one must be different. That is why it is so difficult to find a memorable username when you use a huge email provider.

The part after the @ is called the domain name. As well as telling you the name of the organisation providing the user's email service, it can tell you what type of organisation it is and where in the world it is registered.

If you see '.uk' or '.fr' or '.ru', you are dealing with an organisation registered in Britain, France or Russia. A full list of countries is available from IANA at **www.iana.org/ cctld/cctld.htm**. The part of the domain name that comes just before that is supposed to tell you the type of organisation. In Britain, these include 'co.', 'ltd.', and 'plc.' for businesses, 'org.' for nonprofit organisations, 'sch.' for schools, 'ac.' for higher and further education, 'gov.' for government and 'net.' for organisations concerned with the Internet.

Domain names that have no two-letter country code indicate American or International organisations. These names end in '.com' for businesses, '.org' for nonprofit organisations, '.net' for Internet-related organisations, '.edu' for schools and colleges, '.gov' for the US government and '.mil' for the US military. These codes indicate only that the name has been registered in America, not that it belongs to an American company. Many companies with global ambitions use .com addresses.

The part before '.co.uk' or '.com' is the one-word Internet name of the organisation that owns the site. Here we find the famous corporate names: Tesco, BBC, Microsoft and so on. They must be registered for an annual fee, and details of their ownership kept in various registries around the world. See 'Domain' below for more details.

The domain name can be as simple as 'bt.com', but there can be other 'subdomains' in front of that. For instance, John Smith's email might just as easily be **john@smith.smallprovider.co.uk**. This indicates that a commercial organisation has registered the name smallprovider in Britain. That provider has a computer, or more likely a folder within a computer, called smith. And someone called john keeps their email account in that folder. For that reason, that 'smith', the bit directly adjoining the @, is called the 'host name'.

The domain-name parts of email addresses are also used in the Internet generally, to indicate a website or a file.

When it starts with something like 'http://' or 'ftp://' this type of address is known as a URL, or 'Universal Resource Locator'. Those bits indicate the method that must be used to contact the site or retrieve the file. Thankfully, modern browsers don't require you to use them except in unusual circumstances.

Documents or sites that form part of the World Wide Web generally have addresses that begin 'www' but that is not essential. If you see a site called **smallprovider.com** you may be able to type just that into your browser. The browser will supply the rest to take you to **http:// smallprovider.com**. Usually, though, the site will be found at **www.smallprovider.com**.

That basic version takes visitors only to the reception area of a site. Other pages within the site will have more complex addresses, carrying on after the '.com' or the '.co.uk'. First comes a 'forward slash', and after that comes 'file path'. This is a sort of route map to help the browser find the file: go to a folder called 'home', look inside and find a folder called 'products'; now open that and find a folder called 'images'; open that and there's a file called 'widget.gif'. A picture of a widget: just what you wanted.

Each step in that process is marked off by another forward slash. Like this: **www.widgetpower.com/home/ products/images/widget.gif**.

If you type that in and don't get through, you can always start at the end and whittle each element away, stopping at the next slash mark each time. If you can't get into the folder called 'images', you may be able to get into the folder called 'products' and then find the images folder.

In truth, Internet addresses are so unwieldy that most people do their best to avoid them. To work properly, they have to be typed accurately. While domain names are not case-sensitive (it doesn't matter whether you use capitals or not) the file path may well be.

Modern browsers fill in the 'http://' element. If you are looking for a big American site, you can often just type in the name and the browser will assume you mean www and .com. Try typing in 'Exxon' and see what happens. Some browsers will also 'autocomplete' any address you start typing by checking to see if you have used it in the past.

Mostly, Internet users move from link to link without typing anything. When they find anything they may want to use again, they add it to their browser's 'Bookmarks' or 'Favorites' (spelled the American way). Similarly, email addresses can be copied from incoming correspondence directly into your email address book. Anything to avoid typing those strings of letters and numbers.

The computers themselves don't actually use the URLs and domain names. Each computer on the network has what is called an Internet Protocol (IP) address. These are made up of four numbers, separated by dots, looking like this: 193.128.224.1. When you give your computer an Internet address containing a domain name, your computer looks up the name in an index held at a distant site and finds the IP address so it can connect. If you are using a normal dial-up connection to the Internet, your computer will be given a temporary IP address each time you connect.

AOL

Stands for America On Line, although the service now has a strong presence elsewhere, including Britain. AOL is an online service, meaning it was originally a community of computer users outside the Internet. Today it offers Internet access, but still has special content and forums for members only. It offers reassurance to those starting up on the net, but this can seem restrictive, especially since it has its own proprietary software and standards.

Applet

A small program using the Java language and built into a web page, allowing it to do clever things like show animation, scrolling text, little games and movie clips. Unfortunately, they can cause your browser to crash. They can also leave loopholes that can allow hackers to extract information from your computer. You can disable Java in Preferences in your browser, but increasingly websites expect you to have it.

Article

A contribution to a newsgroup or Usenet group. Covers everything from learned discussion to childish name-calling, just like the newsgroups themselves. Outlook Express and Netscape Messenger can be used for writing newsgroup articles, but regulars prefer dedicated news programs.

ASCII

ASCII stands for American Standard Code for Information Interchange. It means the basic 128 letters, numbers and symbols that can be read by all computers. If a file is in 'ASCII' it is in plain text with no frills. To produce an ASCII document, save it as 'text' in your word processor.

Attachments

Email is not just for sending short notes in text. You can also attach files to your email messages. These can contain pictures, sounds, graphics or anything else. To send an 'attachment', create a new mail message in your mail program. In Outlook Express, click 'add attachments'. A menu will appear: browse through it until you find the file you want. Then click 'choose'. In Netscape Messenger, click 'attach', and when you have found your file, click 'attach'. The attachment then appears in a box above the message you are typing: you will need to say something to explain what it is.

In Outlook Express, the attachment is invisible until you click on a small triangle next to the word 'attachments'. Outlook Express also gives you a number of options for the way the file is sent. This is straightforward unless you are sending your file to a different type of computer: PC, Mac or Unix. You must choose an appropriate type of 'encoding' and 'compression', which shrinks large files. Messenger makes these decisions for you.

Receiving attachments may be more problematical than sending them, because they can carry viruses. Straight data files, containing pictures and words, are less likely to be damaging than those containing programs (with the '.exe' suffix in the PC world), but even Microsoft Word and Excel files can carry viruses if they include 'macros', little programs that automate repetitive tasks.

A virus becomes active only once the file is opened. The best advice is never to open an attachment you are not expecting. If you receive such a 'gift', ask the sender to explain what it is. Even well-intentioned people can accidentally spread viruses. If you decide to open it, move it to a separate folder and let your antivirus program examine it. You do have an antivirus program, don't you? See 'Virus' below for more information. Recently, the antivirus companies claim to have found a rare virus that can be transmitted in HTML email messages, if you are using a particular type of program. If that catches on, life will become very difficult.

Auctions

Auctions have been one of the biggest growth areas in e-commerce. Auction sites offer you the chance to buy and sell anything. You place a description and a picture on the site, set a reserve price below which you won't sell, are given a closing date for the sale and then wait for the bids to come in. The site sends you emails to let you know how the auction is progressing. If you are bidding, you can browse the site or search for specific items. You can even set up a 'robot' to ensure that you continue to bid until you reach a ceiling.

If you win, it is up to you to arrange delivery and payment with the seller, at least in the case of a private auction. But the auction sites also sell commercially, in which case they arrange those things. It is important to remember that any bid you make is legally binding. You also have to register with the site so that they know where you are and can pursue you if you do not keep your side of any bargain. The market leader is the American site eBay (**www.ebay.com**), a slick and impressive operation selling a wide range of goods of all sorts. Its auctions are very busy. It now has a British version: **www.ebay.co.uk**. On this side of the Atlantic the best-known name is QXL (**www.QXL.com**), which has less stock, less activity and a less convincing presentation, although it does have Hugh Scully. Another British example is eBid (**www.eBid.co.uk**), where you can find people hoping to get £1,000 for dull domain names. Online auctions are a phenomenon of our age.

Avatar

A little picture intended to represent you when you visit certain chat rooms. It can be a photograph (not of yourself), a cartoon character or an illustration. It can move around on the screen, interacting with other members of the room. Your 'chat' comes out as speech bubbles. Requires special software. Try it at The Palace (**www.thepalace.com**) or Virtualzones (**www.virtualzones.co.uk**). Beware, some people's 'avatars' are designed to offend.

B

Bandwidth

The rate at which electronic information flows across a connection. Usually expressed in 'bits per second', bandwidth represents the difference between waiting ages for a few pictures to appear and watching full-screen video in comfort. The more bandwidth, the better, but it costs.

BBS

Bulletin board system: a computer to which you dial in for information or to exchange comments. Superseded by the

Internet but still sometimes offered by software and hardware companies.

Binary

A binary file is one that contains anything that is not text: pictures, sounds, programs, video. Can be sent and received over email as an attachment.

Bookmark

A web address stored in the Netscape browser. The same thing in Internet Explorer is called a Favorite (note spelling). You can store a page as a bookmark while you are looking at it by pulling down the 'Bookmarks' or 'Favorites' menu. These menus also allow you to add new bookmarks by writing in their addresses directly, to organise them into groups and folders, and to share them with other people.

It is easy to move 'bookmarks' into Internet Explorer and 'favorites' into Netscape. In Internet Explorer you must first open the Favorites window in the Windows menu. Then you go to File and click 'export': a file called 'favorites.html' is created. Then you start Netscape and go to Edit Bookmarks in the Bookmarks menu. Next you open File and click 'Import . . .' A menu appears: find 'favorites.html', highlight it and click 'open'. Your IE favorites now appear in your Netscape 'bookmarks' list.

Moving your bookmarks to IE is easier, once you have found where they live. You need a file called 'Bookmarks.html'. Then go to the Windows menu of IE, open Favorites, then go to File and click Import Favorites. Find 'Bookmarks.html' and click 'Open'. That's all there is to it.

Bookmark manager

A website that stores your bookmarks and favorites so that you can find them even if you are not using your own computer. Some versions let members share bookmarks to create a sort of directory of well-loved sites. Look at Blink (**www.blink.com**) to see how it works. The Yahoo! search directory offers a similar service.

bps

Bits per second, the unit used to measure the speed at which information passes between two computers. Modern modems can pass information at 56,000 bits per second (56K). The ADSL system can download at between 512 Kbps and 2Mbps (two million bits per second). Remember that eight bits make up one byte, which is what file size is measured in. Don't think your two-megabit-per-second connection will download a two-megabyte file in one second: it will take more than eight times that.

Browser

For people who use the Internet a lot – and that is most people who have tried it – the browser is the most important piece of software they own. Surprisingly, it is usually the one they have paid least for. At least 90 per cent of people will use either Microsoft's Internet Explorer or Netscape Communicator, and both are available free. If you are using Windows or the Mac, you will probably start with the browser that came ready installed, and that invariably means IE.

If you are installing a browser for the first time, or trying the alternative, you can download them from either **www.netscape.com** or **www.microsoft.com/ie**. It's always a better idea to take them from one of those CDs given away each month by the computer magazines.

Each browser has its fans, but which one is better for you depends on which computer you are using.

Each new version adds extra features as the two manufacturers try to take the initiative. The most recent version of Internet Explorer (as I write), IE 5.0, includes a gadget to help you manage Internet auctions. This constant escalation of functions means increasing demands on your computer: if you have an older, slower machine, you will need to use earlier, simpler versions.

Most people would probably settle for stable, fast handling of the basic browser functions: accessing sites, displaying pages, storing pages and bookmarks. Sadly, neither Microsoft nor Netscape seems to make those a priority. Using browsers continues to be a frustrating experience.

For that reason, a few people have sought out browsers from smaller companies, usually because they promise to be faster, more reliable, take up less disk space and use less memory in their computers. For the PC, and soon for the Mac, a browser called Opera has won acclaim: go to traviata.nta.no. For the Mac, consider the German iCab: **www.icab.de**. For most people the drawback is that these programs have to be paid for. Opera costs $35, while iCab will cost $29 when finished, although a free version will also apparently be offered. Anyone taking a serious interest in browsers should go to Browser Watch (**http://browserwatch.internet.com**) for the lowdown.

Perhaps the best advice about browsers is to get to know one inside out before you are tempted to change. Upgrading to a later model should be simple, but is not. And changing to a rival browser can make grown-ups weep.

C

Cache

Your browser stores bits of the web pages you visit in a 'cache' on your computer's hard disk. If you return to that page, it can take them from the hard disk rather than download them, which speeds up the process. You can adjust the size of your cache in both browsers by going to the Edit menu and finding Preferences, then Advanced, then Cache. Most people keep a cache of about 10Mb or 10,480 kilobytes (which is the same thing) if you are using Netscape. While you are there, ensure that the button marked 'Update pages' or 'Page in cache is compared to page on network' is set to 'once per session'. That way your computer starts with an up-to-date copy of a page when you first go to it in any web session. The term is also used by computer hardware manufacturers to mean a memory chip used to speed up processing.

Capitals

Be careful about capital letters. They don't matter in email addresses, but if you use them in web addresses when they are not required you may not get what you are looking for. And in email and newsgroups capital letters are considered to be SHOUTING and consequently unpopular.

Chat

Chat is 'live' conversation over the Internet, but typing rather than speaking. Unlike in a news group, you type something and get a response almost immediately. You can either chat with all the members of a given 'room' or 'channel' or single out one or more people for private discussion. It's a bit like CB radio.

If you want to chat to strangers from all over the world, the traditional system is called Internet Relay Chat (IRC). It requires you to install a small program on your machine (try mIRC or PIRCH for Windows or IRCle for Mac). Then you give yourself a nickname, select a server near you and choose the 'channel' or room in which to begin chatting. Be aware that, as soon as you log on to an IRC chat room, everyone else knows you are there and may expect a contribution. People talk in abbreviations to save time and use smileys (see 'Smiley' below). You may also run into people who want to bully you or practise their hacking skills. A guide to the subject can be found at IRC Help (www.irchelp.org).

Web chat is slower but prettier to look at. Some sites require their own software, but others require you to click 'refresh' or 'reload' to see each new contribution. There are thousands of chat sites offering millions of rooms, often arranged according to geography, interests, age and so on. Once again you will want to choose a nickname, but may also choose an icon or 'avatar' (see above) to represent you. Then chat away, either in the group or on a one-to-one basis.

Remember, always, that you know nothing about the person at the other end and that they may not be telling the truth about themselves.

A useful list of chat sites is available from Yahoo! at http://dir.yahoo.com/Computers_and_Internet/Internet/World_Wide_Web/Chat/. Yahoo also has its own Yahoo! Chat system.

Slightly weirder are the so-called 'virtual worlds', where your avatars move around an animated set as well as chatting. Perhaps the most famous is WorldsAway, now known as Vzone: www.avaterra.com.

If you mainly want to chat with people you know, however, a better bet might be a program called ICQ (it stands for 'I seek you') or the similar Netscape/AOL Instant Messenger. If your friends and colleagues are using the same software, the programs detect when they are online and allows you to chat with them either singly or in groups. You can also chat with strangers if they use the software. Both programs are free, easy to use and surprisingly addictive. As always, be aware of how long you are using the telephone line and how much it is costing you. You can get details of ICQ from www.icq.com. Instant Messenger is available from www.aol.com/aim. You don't have to use Netscape or be an AOL member. ICQ and Instant Messenger can communicate with one another.

Increasingly, written 'chat' is being replaced by the real thing, allowing you to have actual conversations via your computer's sound system and a microphone.

Children

Children are very interested in the Internet, not least because most of their favourite television programmes encourage them to visit their websites or send email. There are also masses of interesting and useful sites dealing with everything from hobbies to homework. See the directory

117

of websites in the next chapter, 'Sites for Sore Eyes', for more details.

But you don't have to look far to see how threatening the Internet can be to children, especially younger ones. Partly it's about what they might see. But the more serious danger comes from contacts they might make. There is no perfect answer to either problem, which is why it makes sense to make Internet use a public, family activity rather than something a child does alone. Even then, you risk embarrassing yourself. The ingenuity of the porn industry is such that even a straightforward search for something harmless can lead you straight to the hard stuff. If you don't fancy explaining what you have stumbled upon, use a search engine with a 'family filter' to screen out the rude words. Most now have them.

Beyond that, there are various technological approaches that can help. The most secure method is to use what is called a 'walled garden'. This is an online area that contains only material guaranteed to be suitable for children. It also controls email and news access. Versions are available from computer makers such as Apple and from various ISPs and interested organisations. They do a good job for younger children, but they mean sacrificing the spirit of open-ended searching that is so much a part of the Internet. You should use a password system to ensure that, while your children are confined to the 'garden', you can step outside when necessary.

A less comprehensive approach is provided by the use of children's search engines and portals. AOL has 'Kids Only' for its members. 'AskJeeves for Kids' (**www.ajkids.com**) and Yahooligans (**www.yahooligans.com**) are available on the web. The human element in their production should mean both that the porn stays out while sensible sites about 'how to tell the sex of a budgerigar' make it in.

This is the home territory of the commercial 'blocking' programmes. Some simply screen out rude words. Others work by measuring the proportion of the screen occupied by flesh tones. Unfortunately, these are crude devices. In order to achieve their usual promise of blocking 95 per cent of explicit material, they also block large numbers of inoffensive sites. They ban things that some Americans find offensive but don't disturb us, for instance astrology. They often have religious and political biases you may not share. And they certainly won't stop an ingenious teenager – but by then it is probably too late to worry. The leading brands are CYBERsitter (**www.solidoak.com**), Net Nanny (**www.netnanny.com**), Cyber Patrol (**www.cyberpatrol. com**) and SurfWatch (**www.surfwatch.com**). They cost between $29.95 and $49.95, depending on whether you download them or buy a CD, and only Cyber Patrol and Surfwatch are available for the Mac.

Your browser has its own built-in censorship system, which you can access through 'Ratings' in the Preferences menu. It allows you to set the levels of sex, violence, nudity and bad language you want to allow through. Sites assess their own levels of offensiveness and label themselves invisibly. Your browser then warns you about the site and bans access to it if it is above a level of nastiness you have previously set. To make this work with older children, you will need to use a password to stop them disabling it in the browser's Preferences.

The worst that can happen with the web is that your children see something frightening or unwelcome. But more serious problems have arisen with email and with chat. Children with email addresses will certainly receive the same sexually explicit junk emails as everyone else. They may be approached by strangers. And because users of the Internet can claim to be anyone they like, intense email or chat relationships that threaten to turn into real relationships can be dangerous. Some blocking software will send all your children's email via you. Others will block the passing on of potentially dangerous material, such as phone numbers, addresses and credit-card details. Others limit chat to rooms with adult monitoring and exclude the newsgroups altogether.

Once again there is no substitute for being with your children when they are learning about the net and talking to them about the dangers. You should ensure they don't provide personal details or arrange any sort of meeting. Kids like Internet chat, but it has no great educational value and will be no sacrifice, especially if you are paying for your Internet connection time.

Client
Your computer, if you are contacting another computer over the Internet or any other network. Also the software – usually a browser – that allows your computer to be a client.

Compressed file
Files are squeezed to take up less space and so less time when they are transmitted across the Internet. Then they must be uncompressed with, for instance, WinZip for Windows (**www.winzip.com**) or Stuffit Expander (**www. aladdinsys.com**).

Control Panel(s)
You can, if you are brave, fiddle about with the way your computer communicates with the Internet. In Windows, go to Settings in the Start Menu and open Control Panel: there you will find lots of icons full of things that can be adjusted. The relevant ones are Modems (there may also be one including the name of your actual modem) and Internet Settings. On the Mac, go to the Apple menu, call up Control Panels, and then look for Internet, Modem, Remote Access and TCP/IP. The best advice is not to touch any of these unless you have to, perhaps when changing your ISP or your modem. But then you should have some technical support to talk you through the process.

The safe exceptions to the hands-off policy are: turning off the nasty sound of your modem (click Properties in the

Modems panel in Windows, or open Modem in the Mac); ensuring you have a blank home page in your browser and that it refreshes stored pages only once per session (in Internet Settings in Windows, but only through your browser's Preferences in Mac); and changing your ISP's phone number (in Windows, go to Internet Settings, then Connections. Then highlight the name of your provider, then click Settings and finally a tab marked Properties. Then you can change the number. In the Mac, go to Remote Access and you should see the number you need to change).

Cookie

A cookie is a small text file that allows a web site to know that you have previously visited. At the very least, it allows online shops to greet you by name. People worry about whether they infringe your privacy, but they store only information you have supplied, for instance when registering with a site. Unfortunately, ingenious advertisers have worked out ways to 'track' your progress around the web and send you personalised advertising based on what you have been looking at. Those who don't like the implications of this can delete their cookies or refuse to accept any more by going to their browser Preferences and clicking on Cookies. The drawback is that sites will keep asking you to accept them. And, of course, your favourite shops won't recognise you. More information from Cookie Central (www.cookiecentral.com). And see 'Privacy' below.

Crash

All computer programs crash, freeze, hang and fail to function at some point. Browser software is worse than most. If you must browse while other programs and documents are open, save them before you start. When your browser crashes or freezes, or the pointer disappears, you may have to restart the computer, and then anything not saved will be lost.

If the browser window is visible but not working, try

quitting the program. That probably won't work. Then, in Windows, try pressing CTRL-ALT-DEL (that's control, alt and delete at the same time). That should bring up a window that will allow you to close just the browser without restarting the computer, but you will probably want to do that anyway, just to be safe. A second jab at CTRL-ALT-DEL will close the machine down.

On the Mac, hold down the Apple (command) key, option and esc. That may allow you to close just the browser: but the computer will most likely freeze, forcing you to restart by holding down the power switch or using the restart button on older models.

Cyberspace
A romantic term for the world created by computers and the information they contain. Coined by William Gibson in his novel *Neuromancer*.

D

Decompress
Some files are compressed to make them smaller and thus quicker to send across the Internet. You use a program such as WinZip or Aladdin Expander to decompress them at your end.

Diary sites
Rather than keep your own personal or work schedule on your own computer (or in a pocket diary), you can keep it on a website designed for the purpose. It means that if you forget your diary you can access your schedule from anywhere you can find a computer. It also means you can make your diary available to other people, so they can check your availability without having to ask. On the other hand, it is one more password to remember.

Try the British Diary Manager (**www.diarymanager.com**) or use the daily web planner at **www.dwp.net** for the basic service. More elaborate versions, including to-do lists, are available from Joint Planning (**www.jointplanning.com**) and the Windows-only Visto (**www.visto.com**). An interesting twist comes from When.com (**www.when.com**), which lets you integrate your diary with its extensive calendar of arts and business events – sadly, it is entirely US-based.

Directory

Search sites on the web come in two basic sorts: search engines, which try to find certain words within websites, and directories or searchable subject indexes. Directories try to put the contents of the web into categories. To find things, you can start by looking at broad categories and then work your way down to much narrower ones. For instance, Yahoo!, the most famous directory, has categories called 'Arts & Humanities', 'Business & Economy', 'Computers & Internet', 'Recreation and Sport' and so on. Click on 'Recreation and Sport', for instance, and you find a further list of categories. Click 'Outdoor', then 'Bungee Jumping', and eventually you will find a list of bungee-jumping sites, with British examples marked with a Union Jack. You can speed the process up by typing the thing you are looking for into the search box at the top of each page: but remember that it searches subject headings, not actual pages. That will take you to one of its categories.

Compared with the number of sites unearthed by a search engine, directories are small and select. And selections are often made by humans, rather than computers. This makes them useful for some types of search: for instance, if you are looking for lots of sites on the same general topic, rather than something specific.

Naturally, some of the search-engine companies have caught on. AltaVista and Google now both offer directories, based on the volunteer-edited Open Directory project, although Google buries its directory: find it by clicking where it says 'or browse web pages by category'. AltaVista's also uses the resources of LookSmart (**www.looksmart. com**), a similar service to Yahoo!.

Better than all these, for those who like the human touch, is About (www.about.com), which is a directory with 700 subject areas individually selected by named editors, pictured on the site.

Document
Any sort of file you can receive or send across the Internet, including words, spreadsheets, databases, pictures, sounds and video.

Domain
A domain is the key part of an Internet address. A domain name usually consists of a company or organisation name, separated by a dot from something that identifies its nature or the place where it was registered. Thus **whotsit. com** might be the domain of a commercial company called Whotsit, registered in the US. The bit after the dot, called the 'top-level domain', indicates American-registered educational ('edu'), government ('gov'), Internet ('net'), non-profit ('org') or military ('mil') organisations. Two-letter abbreviations indicate countries: 'uk' for Britain, 'de' for Germany, 'fr' for France and so on. Usually another abbreviation is inserted before the country code, giving us 'co.uk', 'gov.uk', 'org.uk' and more recently 'plc.uk' and 'ltd.uk'. But it need not be. The British Library, for instance, is **www.bl.uk**.

There may be other names or abbreviations, divided by dots, before the real domain name, as in **screaming. abdabs.co.uk**. 'Screaming' here is a subdomain, one division or subsidiary of the main abdabs domain. The bit that comes immediately after the 'www' or the 'http://' is known as the host, since that is where the information in question is actually kept: **www.screaming.abdabs.co.uk**. If it is an email address, the name of the user replaces the 'www': **jones@screaming.abdabs.co.uk**.

Unfortunately the top-level domain codes are increasingly meaningless, since companies with global ambitions like to be called '.com', and other people have found that there is fun to be had with such suffixes as '.to' and '.it'. But domain names have to be bought and registered, and it is usually possible to find out who owns or registered them, even if that proves to be only an agent.

The Internet's computers don't actually use the domain names. They use a string of numbers. Computers called Domain Name Servers supply the right numbers when your machine sends them a domain name. Sometimes your browser will announce a 'Failed DNS lookup'. This means that the Domain Name Server can't find a number to match your written name. Try clicking 'reload' or 're-fresh': otherwise, you may just have typed it incorrectly.

Downloading

Every time you go to a web page or collect your email, you download things to your computer (sending things the other way is called uploading). But when people talk about downloading they generally mean collecting large files that take many minutes or even hours to crawl over the Internet to your desktop. There are innumerable things to download in this way, particularly programs, whether free, shareware (meaning you pay a modest fee) or fully commercial, stored on such sites as Download.com (**http://download.cnet.com**), Shareware.com (**http://shareware.cnet.com**) and TUCOWS (**www.tucows.com**).

Your browser will download them to your hard disk, usually in compressed form: their names will have a .zip or (on the Mac) a .sit suffix. Even so, the process is slow. With a normal 56k modem, it will take about five minutes to download a 1Mb file. To open them you will need a decompressing program, but those are often installed when you get your computer. If not, go to **www.winzip.com** and **www.aladdinsys.com** to get the most popular decompressing tools for Windows. Aladdin also makes the basic Stuffit program that comes with the Mac.

People who do this kind of thing a lot might prefer to use

a dedicated FTP (file transfer protocol) program rather than use the browser. For one thing, they can always restart after your connection has broken without losing anything. Also, they make sense if you want to 'upload' things. You can do that with Netscape, but not with Internet Explorer.

Downloads, particularly of programs, are a potential source of viruses, but good FTP sites know they need to keep their catalogue infection-free if they are to stay in business. Ensure you have some kind of antivirus software and that it is up to date.

E

eBay
Impressive and successful American online auction site that has spawned many imitators. Now has its own British site: www.ebay.co.uk.

Email
Also spelled 'e-mail' or 'E-mail'. Email is a system for sending text messages from computer to computer over telephone lines. Many people find it the most useful part of the whole Internet. You can send a message across the world without leaving your desk and for the price of a brief local phone call. If you type the address properly, your message always gets through, with no engaged tones or being put on hold. You can send messages at night for people to read first thing in the morning. You can send not only words but pictures, sounds or anything else that can be put in digital form. And it's fun: before you know it you'll have email friends all over the world.

You will need to agree an email address with whoever is providing your Internet service. It will probably resemble your own name, but you can have lots more from different services if you find that restrictive. You will also need a 'mail client', the program that lets you send, receive and store emails. Most people use the one that comes with their favourite browser, which means either Microsoft's Outlook Express or Netscape's Messenger.

Incoming email is held in your 'mailbox' at your Internet provider until you dial up to collect it. You will need a password for that, although your computer will usually store it for you and submit it automatically. You can arrange to receive product updates and email magazines, and you will certainly get junk email (often known as spam).

Your outgoing mail can be dressed up with different fonts and type styles by your browser, if you choose the 'HTML' option. Some browsers even include a selection of little pictures. These are not always appreciated by recipients because they are slow to download. More usefully you can send documents, graphics, photographs and sound as 'attachments' with email.

Sending email is as simple as clicking on the 'new message' in the File menu, then typing the address alongside the word 'to:'. It is here that most emails go astray, which is why most people maintain a large 'address book' in their browser. Then you can either select a name from that or start typing and let the program try to fill it in for you if it is an address you have used before. Then type in a 'subject': sensible subject headings help email users sort out real messages from junk.

When you receive emails, you can ask the program to add the sender's address to your address book. Look under Message in Netscape and Tools in Outlook Express. Of course, if someone writes to you, you can reply simply by clicking the reply button. If you click reply, the subject will be the original subject with 'Re:' in front of it.

It is common practice to quote back things people have said in your reply: this helps them keep track of your correspondence. Depending on how you set them up, both mail programs will automatically copy the original message into your reply. The original is marked off by angled brackets at the beginning of each line. It's also in a different colour.

Your mail messages can be sent to many recipients simultaneously by clicking the CC (carbon copy) tab when you write your message: if you don't want recipients to see the list of who else received it, use BCC (blind carbon copy).

If you are paying for your online time, it makes sense to read and write your email when you are not connected. Mail programs and browsers tend to assume your connection is permanent and free. Consequently they have to be configured to prevent them dialling up when you open the program, when you complete a message and when you close the program. In Outlook Express, go to Tools and look under Schedules. In Netscape, go to Preferences, then Offline, where you can ensure that the program doesn't connect until you tell it to.

If you just want an email account, or you want an extra one, there are plenty of ways you can get one for nothing, provided you are prepared to accept a certain amount of advertising. The most celebrated is Microsoft's Hotmail (www.hotmail.com), which works through a web page rather than your email program. You can sign up through a menu item in Outlook Express. Other 'portal' sites, Yahoo!, Escape, Netscape, offer the same service without that refinement.

But you can also get free email using the 'traditional' POP3 system, or use a 'remailer' to redirect your mail so that you can have a new email address while keeping your old account. There is a list of more than 1,000 free email services and lots of useful information at the Free Email Address Directory (www.emailaddresses.com).

Email address

An email address is instantly recognisable because somewhere in the middle the @ symbol will appear, followed by the host and domain name where the mailbox is stored. Email addresses are not case-sensitive: you don't have to worry about using capital letters or not.

CompuServe and AOL have their own system for email

between members, but they can be converted for Internet use. CompuServe number 100345,1425 becomes **100345. 1425@compuserve.com**. AOL member names simply acquire the @aol.com suffix like this: **dave@AOL.com**.

Encryption

Encryption is a way of encoding information passing around the web so that it cannot be read without being decoded. It is the technology behind the little 'padlock' symbol that appears in your browser when you access a 'secure' site. It makes sure that both ends of the transaction are who they say they are, and that the information passing between them cannot be read by anyone else. This is essential for banking and shopping where credit-card details are used.

Some individuals apply encryption to their own private correspondence and their own hard disks, using a widely available program called PGP (Pretty Good Privacy). A basic explanation of how to use it – though not how it works, luckily – is available from the Web Developer's Journal: **http://webdevelopersjournal.co.uk/articles/pgp.htm**. More serious information, and the program itself, is available from The International PGP Home Page (**www.pgpi.org**).

Error messages

Sometimes, when you try to go to a website, all you get is a very plain screen with an error message on it. First try clicking the 'Refresh' or 'Reload' button once or twice. If that doesn't work, check that you have typed or copied the site's address properly. The 'file paths' of web addresses are case-sensitive, meaning any capital letters must be in the right place. Make sure that you didn't type commas instead of full stops or use backslashes instead of forward slashes.

If you copied the URL and pasted it into the browser's address slot, make sure you copied the whole thing: a '**ww.something.com**' or '**ttp://whotnot.co.uk**' address will always bring up an error message. If none of that works, you can try whittling down the address step by step.

Taking away everything after the final slash (/) will mean you won't get straight to the file you want, but you'll go to the directory or folder that contains it. If that doesn't work, delete that directory name and try to go to a higher-level folder until you eventually get back to the main domain name.

Error messages come in many different styles, but they include several standard codes.

400 Bad request: The page you want does not exist or the URL is wrong.

401 Unauthorised: This page is password-protected. Either you don't have the password or you have typed it wrongly.

403 Forbidden: The same as unauthorised.

404 Not found: The page doesn't exist, or you have the wrong URL. The error could be as simple as typing '.htm' instead of '.html'.

503 Service unavailable: The equivalent of an engaged tone. Try again in a few seconds.

Host unknown: The site may have moved or changed its name. You can probably find it via a search engine, which may have a more recent domain name.

Host unavailable: The host computer is not working at the moment. Try later.

File contains no data: A blank page, but it may be temporary. Try later.

Bad file request: An error found when completing online forms. Your browser may not support that type of form, or it may be written wrongly.

Too many connections: Site overloaded by traffic. Click Reload/Refresh or try later.

Connection refused by host: You don't have the right password.

Failed DNS lookup: The URL you have typed does not match anything on the Internet. Try Reload/Refresh or check that you filled in the address/location properly. If you get it all the time, you may need to reconfigure your computer's control panels, using a DNS number supplied by your Internet provider.

Helper application not found: The file you have asked for requires your browser to use a helper application that you don't have. Download the appropriate helper, or forget it.

F

FAQ

Frequently Asked Questions. One great invention of the Internet world is the idea of passing on basic information through questions and answers. You will find FAQs on websites, in equipment manuals, in the help files of programs and in newsgroups, which is where they originated. Every newsgroup has an FAQ, to set out the group's interests and to stop people asking the same questions over and over again: you can look at many of them, and lots of other interesting stuff, at the Internet FAQ Archives (**www.faqs.org**).

Favorite

The equivalent of a Bookmark in Microsoft's Internet Explorer: note the US spelling. 'Bookmarks' is the more widely used term outside the IE context.

File types

Every document or file created by a computer has a name. The first part is to identify it: the second part, the 'suffix', which comes after a dot, says what type of document it is or what program created it. Thus trousers.doc is a document called 'trousers' created in a word processor, probably Microsoft Word. Your particular computer system may not show you the suffixes, but they are there.

As you see and download different pages, with different features, you will come across lots of different file types. A vast list of the file-type suffixes can be seen at **www.whatis. com/ff.htm** but here are a few of the common or problematical ones:

.aif and .aiff = sound files used by Macintosh programs.

.arc or .arj = compressed archive file for the PC.

.asc = an ASCII text file.

.asp = active server page, meaning a web page containing a small program.

.bin = a Mac binary file, expanded automatically by Macs, or can be expanded using Stuffit Expander.

.bmp = a Windows graphics file.

.cgi = common gateway interface, a script built into a web page.

.css = a cascading style sheet, used to format web pages.

.doc = Microsoft Word or similar word processor file.

.drv = a driver file needed for a modem, printer or other device.

.eps = encapsulated post script, a graphics file that will work only on a PostScript printer.

.exe = an 'executable' program file in Windows. Potential virus hazard.

.gif = a graphics file, often used for line art, clip art and cartoons.

.hqx = a compressed file for Macintosh, to be opened with Stuffit Expander.

.html and .htm = web pages written in HTML.

.jpeg, .jpe, .jfif, .jff, .jif = compressed graphics files, usually of photographs.

.kar = karaoke file using the MIDI system to generate sound and lyrics.

.mid = MIDI music file.

.mime, .mme, .mim = email attachment file.

.mov, .movie, .moov = movie clip that requires Quick-Time.

.mp3 = compressed sound file.

.mpeg = animation or movie file.

.pdf = a portable document format file to be viewed with Acrobat.

.png = compressed graphics file.

.ps = PostScript file, needs a PostScript printer.

.qt = movie file needing QuickTime.

.ra and .ram = sound files needing Real Audio player.

.rtf = word processing file understood by most WP programs.

.sea = compressed Mac file that expands itself.

.tif, .tiff = graphics files.

.txt = plain ASCII text file.

.wav = sound file for Windows.

.wmf = a file used to display a picture in Windows.

.zip = compressed file that must be expanded using WinZip.

Flaming

Abusive contributions to newsgroups or mailing lists. Sometimes people contribute provocative 'flame bait' to provoke a 'flame war'.

Frames

Way of creating a web page that divides the screen into sections, each of which is really a separate page. You can switch your browser's ability to recognise frames on or off in Preferences, which may speed up browsing. But some sites can be viewed only with a browser that recognises frames. When attempting to save a page with frames to your hard disk, it is essential to ensure that you are saving the right frame. It is sometimes necessary to open that frame in a new window first by holding down the right button on your mouse (or keeping the button held down in the Mac) and choosing that option in the menu.

FTP

File transfer protocol: the system used to move large files backwards and forwards to the Internet. If you see a link or address that begins ftp:// you know that will download a file to your computer. Browsers now have built-in FTP programs, and the process is automated: all you do is click on the link and the browser does the rest. If the link or address ends with a .zip or .exe or similar filename, it goes directly to the file. If it ends with a forward slash (/), you will be in a directory or page of files and will have to search for the precise file you want.

Downloads can take a long time, and your connection is likely to break. Both main browsers are supposed to allow you to resume where you left off, but don't work as reliably as dedicated FTP programs. For Windows, an excellent FTP download helper is Go!Zilla (**www.gozilla.com**). You will certainly need a real FTP program if you intend to upload any large files. For Windows, consider CuteFTP (**www.cuteftp.com**) or WS_FTP (**www.ipswitch.com**). For Mac try Fetch (**www.dartmouth.edu/pages/softdev/fetch. html**) or Anarchie (**www.stairways.com/anarchie/**). Some of these are shareware, some commercial. All will cost between $25 and $40. Free FTP programs are available but have drawbacks. Search TUCOWS (**www.tucows.com**) for 'ftp'.

FTP sites

The Internet has thousands of huge archives of software made available to be downloaded by FTP. There is no charge for downloading, but many will require payment for use. Some of the sites are presented in a familiar web-page format, but others look like old-fashioned computer directories with lots of little folders on screen. The problem is finding them. A searchable index is maintained at **http:// tile.net/ftp-list/,** but it gives only an idea of the types of files the site holds. You have to go to a likely site and look again. Freely available stuff tends to be in a directory called 'pub/' and you may also find a file called 'ls-lR', which contains a list of the site's contents. If you are interested in FTP you should get a file called **ftp://ftp.landfield.com/usenet/news.answers/ ftp-list/ faq** (by FTP, naturally).

G

Games

Increasingly computer games involve the Internet. You can download demos to play at home. If you buy a game, you will often be able to download various add-ons and improvements from the manufacturer's website.

If the game supports it, you can play with and against other people, using the Internet. You will need to go to a gaming site and download the special software that tells you about other people who want to play and connects you to them. Sites worth looking at include Kali (**www.kali.net**), which has software for Macs as well as Windows, Heat (**www.heat.net**), Won.net (**www.uk.won.net**) and Wireplay (**www.wireplay.com**). You must own the full version of the game you want to play: these sites just connect you with other players.

These sites will often also sell you games and let you download demos. Others specialise in simpler games that you can play via your web browser without having to buy anything. These range from classics like chess and draughts to gambling and trivia games and basic arcade-type efforts. Won.net has some, or there are American sites such as Pogo.com (**www.pogo.com**) and Microsoft's Zone.com (**www.zone.com**). Browser-based games are increasingly common on websites aimed at children: look at LEGO.com (**www.lego.com**) or the BBC's *Blue Peter* site at **www.bbc.co.uk/bluepeter/**, for example.

One final area of gaming activity is the world of the fantasy role-playing game. These unfathomable text-based adventures were among the first games played on computers and they are still going strong. Information from The Mud Connector (**www.mudconnector.org**).

Gif

Pronounced 'giff' or 'jiff', this is a common type of graphics file that can be viewed in any browser. May be a photograph or painted graphic.

Gopher

A system for organising information on the Internet, now almost completely replaced by the World Wide Web. Gopher pages keep information inside folders, inside other folders and so on. Your browser will access gopher sites, which have addresses that look like this: **gopher://gopher. uwm.edu**.

H

Hacker

Originally a computer expert who knew how to do clever and useful things with hardware and software. Now usually used for someone who breaks into other people's computers with destructive intent. Purists call these people 'crackers'.

Handle

A nickname, especially in Chat.

Helper

A small program that does a specialised job that the normal browsers can't cope with. If a page includes a specialised animation, sound or video file, your browser will either start the helper program running or suggest how you can get it, usually by downloading it.

History

A list of all the sites you have visited recently: you can click on any of them to save you retyping. Find it on the toolbar or under the Window menu in Internet Explorer. In Netscape, go to the Communicator window, click Tools and finally History. Netscape holds history going back a certain number of days; IE keeps a certain number of sites. Both allow you to wipe the list to help preserve your privacy if others use your machine. Don't use Netscape on the Mac if History is important to you: it stores it only for your current session.

Home page

Ambiguous term meaning any of the following: a modest web page belonging to an individual; the opening page of a larger and more elaborate website (better known as the start page); the page you set your browser to start from. Don't use the home page that comes preselected when you get your browser. It will want to dial up as soon as you start the program.

Host

The computer, or computer directory, that you reach when your browser finds the site or page it is looking for.

Hotmail

Microsoft's web-based email system. You don't need an email program, and no money changes hands: you can open an account instantly using any name you like to send and receive email from the web. Details from **www.hotmail. com**. Similar facilities are now offered by most ISPs and search engine sites. Good fun, but **johnsmith@hotmail.com** is not the most respectable of email addresses.

HTML

Hyper Text Markup Language, the system used to create web pages. It is not difficult to learn and requires no special software, but making it look good and function well is more complicated. If you are saving a page from the web, you can save it 'as HTML source' or 'As Source', depending on which browser you are using. That gets you the words and the layout, but not the pictures. If you want the pictures as well, save as 'Web archive' in Internet Explorer. In Netscape you have to save the pictures separately, one at a time.

If you want to see what a page's HTML code looks like, go to the View menu and select Source or View Source. Sometimes this is the only way to extract information from a badly designed page: for instance if the text is illegible because of its size and colour. It does happen.

HTTP
Hyper Text Transport Protocol: the rules for exchanging information across the web. The full URL of any web page or document will begin with 'http://'.

Hyperlinks
Words, often underlined, that you click on to be taken to another page or document. Pictures and graphics can also be used as hyperlinks.

Hypertext
Words that you click to move to another document or another part of the same document. The basic organisational principle of the web.

I

ICQ
A free program for a special simplified version of Internet chat. It tells you when other users of the system are connected so you can send them messages and get an immediate reply. You can chat one to one or in groups of friends or with complete strangers among the system's 50 million members around the world. Installs a comprehensive communication 'dashboard' on your desktop. Details from **www.icq.com**.

ICU
Pronounced I See You. A program used to create a video chat system, whereby people can see each other as they communicate via computer. From **www.icuii.com**.

Instant Messenger
Also known as AOL Instant Messenger, and included in full installations of Netscape, this is a similar system to ICQ. It also claims to have 50 million users. You do not have to belong to AOL or even to use Netscape. It also offers a way of transferring files without using FTP. Despite AOL's ownership of ICQ, the two systems are not

100 per cent compatible. There is also a Microsoft equivalent, but AOL has refused to open its system so it will communicate with the Microsoft program. Details from **www.aol.com/aim**.

Internet
Once known as the Network of Networks. A system developed by the American military to connect its various individual computer installations, subsequently handed over for civilian use. Until recently it was largely academic in focus and commercialism was scorned.

Internet telephony
A way of using your computer, with a suitable microphone and speakers, to make telephone calls using the Internet. That way an overseas call costs no more than a local call. But quality and reliability are still variable. Some chat and instant messaging systems permit spoken conversations.

Intranet
A private version of the Internet, linking computers belonging to one company or organisation.

IP
Internet Protocol: the rules that control the transmission of data around the Internet.

IP address
A unique number assigned to every computer on the Internet: it consists of four groups of numbers between one and 255, separated by dots. If you are dialling up to an ISP, you will be awarded a temporary IP number from a store that it holds.

IRC
Internet Relay Chat: the program and system used in traditional Internet chat.

ISDN

Integrated Services Digital Network: a system for faster Internet access through ordinary phone lines. In its BT Home Highway version, it ran at twice the speed of normal telephone access, but required simultaneous use of two lines.

ISP

Universal abbreviation for Internet service provider. These are the companies that give home users 'dial-up' access to the Internet, as well as hosting their email mailboxes and their web pages. ISPs are broadly divided into three: paid-for, free and those that pay your telephone bill. Their performance is closely monitored by the Internet magazines. Take a look at *.net* (**www.netmag.co.uk**), *Internet* magazine (**www.internet-magazine.com**), *The Net* (**www.thenetmag.co.uk**) and similar titles before you commit yourself. Only *Internet* magazine puts its ISP listings on its site. Bear in mind that your email address and your home page if you make one will normally feature the ISP's name. Being **jim@nuttyprovider.com** may seem amusing, but will it enhance your career in chartered accountancy?

J

Java

A computer language used to produce special effects and facilities on a web page. Java 'applets' – small applications – work by being downloaded to a suitably equipped browser: most are. Then they crash it. Well, not always, but more often than most users would like. Java can be switched off in the browser's Preferences panel, but a lot of sites insist upon it.

JavaScript

A way of doing browser tricks of various sorts by special programming of a web page. Used for 'ticker' displays of news, special effects and making windows pop up. Mostly harmless, but it can theoretically be used by hackers to find a way into people's private files.

JPEG
A picture file in a format devised by the Joint Picture Experts Group – hence the name. Often used for photographs.

K

Keyword
You use keywords in Internet search engines to help you find things. Type into the search box any words you feel are likely to appear in anything written about the subject you are trying to find. The search engine will normally bring up pages that have all the words first, then those that have some or just one.

Kilobyte
Usually thought of as a thousand bytes, it actually means 1024 bytes for reasons to do with binary arithmetic. A page of plain text is about 8Kbytes.

L

Link
Also known as a hyperlink, this is a word, phrase or picture in a web page that makes something happen when you click on it. Your browser may take you to a new page or open a new window with the new page in it. Or it may show you a picture, play a sound, open a form or bring up a new email message for you to fill in. Originally links were underlined and in a different colour from ordinary text or pictures. Now they can be more difficult to find. Most web sites include a set of useful links to other sites.

Log in/log on
To enter a computer system, either on your desktop or at the other end of a telephone line, usually by typing a

username and password. The username itself is sometimes known as your login or logon, and is not a secret.

Lurk

To observe what goes on in a newsgroup or mailing list without taking part. Despite the unattractive name, this is considered preferable to throwing your weight around before you know what's really going on.

Lycos

Long-established search directory site that now offers many other facilities. Go to **www.lycos.com** or **www. lycos.co.uk** to try it.

M

Mailbox

When you set up an email account, your incoming mail is held by your ISP until you dial up to collect it. You will need a username and a password. If you also know the name used by your ISP's mail server, usually something like **pop.isp.co.uk**, you can collect your mail and respond to it from anywhere with web access by using a site like Mail2Web (**www.mail2web.com**).

Mailing list

Mailing lists send you material by email, if you subscribe. Some are private, some are established by software or hardware companies for commercial purposes, and some are open for the contributions of their subscribers. You may be offered either all the contributions submitted to the list individually every day, which may mean a heavy load of email, or a 'digest' at less frequent intervals. Discussions tend to be more sensible than in the newsgroups, not least because mailing lists are usually 'moderated', meaning supervised. Search for details of available lists – and they cover most subjects – at Liszt (**www.liszt.com**).

Metasearch

A search tool that searches other search engines. This means you may get the top ten answers from ten different search sites. Can operate from a website, such as Izquick (www.izquick.com) or Dogpile (www.dogpile.com), or from a program on your own computer, such as Copernic (www.copernic.com) or Apple's Sherlock II (www.apple.com/sherlock).

MIDI

Musical Instrument Digital Interface: a system for controlling synthesisers from computers. A MIDI file (suffix '.mid' or '.midi') does not store sounds. It is the computer equivalent of one of those paper rolls used to make pianolas and barrel-organs play. It tells the synthesiser what notes to play, in what order, for how long and how loud.

When you download or play a MIDI file on the web, a MIDI plug-in attached to your browser turns the computer into a synthesiser. Or you can use the computer to drive a more sophisticated synthesiser. Depending on your equipment and the way the original file was created, the results can range from tinkly Muzak to astonishing realism. With some software, you can adjust the sounds allocated to the different musical tracks, and rewrite the tracks yourself. You can also get programs that will turn MIDI files into crude but useful sheet music. For the musically inclined, it is great fun.

But, because MIDI does not record sound, no MIDI file will include vocals. If you want a very simple guide to playing MIDI files on your computer look at Charles Kelly's excellent site, starting with **www.aitech.ac.jp/~ckelly/midi/help/**. He also has a remarkable searching page to help you find your favourite tunes: everything from 'Anarchy in the UK' to 'Jerusalem'. Bear in mind that modern music is covered by copyright and should not be reproduced in this way without permission.

Modem

However you access the Internet, you will normally be using a modem (*mo*dulator/*dem*odulator) to turn your equipment's digital signals into sounds that will travel over the telephone wires. 'Internal' modems now come supplied as standard with computers, and a speed of 56Kb (56,000 bits per second) is the maximum achievable. Older computers can benefit from the addition of a faster modem, since speeds have increased in the last few years. The new digital systems for access to the Internet, ISDN and ADSL, don't use modems: they send digital signals down the telephone wire. Nonetheless, the word 'modem' is widely used for any device that sends information through to the Internet.

MP3

System for compressing music files so they take up a reduced amount of space. This makes it possible to send them fairly swiftly over the Internet and to store vast numbers on an ordinary computer hard disk. They can be played back on the computer or on Walkman-style portable MP3 players. Sound is acceptable for portable use but not CD quality. Your system will probably be able to play MP3 files using either the latest versions of QuickTime or the Windows media player. To make the files from your own music or from CDs, you need what is called an MP3 'ripper'. Search **www.tucows.com** or similar using MP3 as your search term.

MPEG

A file containing moving pictures and/or sounds, using a format devised by the Motion Picture Experts Group. Hence the name. Your browser uses a plug-in to play them: usually Apple's QuickTime.

Music

The web has a vast amount of musical material, ranging from newsgroups and mailing lists discussing various bands to vast files of pirated music. Those interested in playing music will be interested in pursuing the MIDI route, which turns musical information into computer code that can be downloaded and played back through your browser – it can sound rather cheesy – or with additional synthesiser equipment. The files, which are the instructions for making sound rather than the sounds themselves, can also be manipulated and processed indefinitely in music programs and even turned into written scores. Those who are more interested in listening will try MP3s. These are standard audio recordings, squeezed to make them small enough to travel over the Internet. Even then, they can take a long time to download: a four-minute track takes up about 3.5Mb. Then they can be stored on your hard disk or downloaded to your MP3 player, if you have one.

MP3 technology is very controversial, with artists going to law to stop the unlimited swapping of their songs. To do this, people used a program called Napster, which locates songs on other users' hard disks and facilitates downloading. The US courts are pondering its legality. For the less contentious end of MP3, involving unsigned bands and those who have given permission for their material to be used, go to www.mp3.com.

N

Napster
Possibly the most controversial piece of software yet developed, Napster lets you instantly find album tracks and then download them for nothing from other people's hard disks (with their permission). But the owners of CDs have no legal right to distribute the music in this way, and at the time of going to press, Napster had indeed been shut down by the US courts. Details from www.napster.com or, for the Mac, www.macster.com. Both work frighteningly well. The same technique has recently been applied to other digital material, notably programs, in a piece of

software called Freenet (**www.freenet.com**), which should provoke even more legal trouble.

Netiquette

Cute name for the 'etiquette' of the net. Should not be taken too seriously, but in newsgroups, chat and email, it usually includes the following advice:

- Read the FAQ: don't ask silly questions.
- Stick to the point: make sure what you have to say is relevant to the group.
- Use a sensible heading so people know whether to read or not.
- Be careful about jokes. They may not work in print, or may offend people in other countries.
- Don't advertise and don't spam (sending the same message to lots of groups or as junk email).
- Stay relaxed: don't be personally abusive.
- Don't type everything in capital letters: it's considered SHOUTING.
- Remember, everything you type in a newsgroup is likely to be archived, so be careful what you say.

Newbie

A less than friendly term for someone new to the Internet, particularly used in areas such as Chat and the Usenet newsgroups, where old hands tend to dominate. It helps to 'lurk' for a while to find out what is going on, to read any available FAQs – regulars dislike discussing the same questions over and over again – and to practise in a 'newbie' area first. IRC, the chat system, has channels or chatrooms just for this purpose: #new2irc, #newuser and #newbies. Usenet has **alt.newbie** and **alt.newbies**, which are full of people sending 'this is a test' messages and also of people giving advice. Or look in **news.newusers.questions**, a 'moderated' group with someone deciding whether contributions should be allowed. Its home page can be found at **http://www.ptialaska.net/ ~kmorgan/** or **www.plig.net/nnq/nnqlinks.html**.

In general, the Internet is tolerant of newcomers: after all, no one has been using it for more than a few years.

Newsgroups

Also known as Usenet, these are discussion groups on the Internet. To read the newsgroups, you use your mail program or special 'newsreader' software. First download the complete list from your ISP's news server. The 'discussions' in question cover most subjects imaginable and a few that are not. Most ISPs will remove some of them. Because no one monitors, edits or referees these discussions, there are no restrictions on subject matter or language. Some of the groups are used for exchanging material that is not legal in most countries. Most of the Internet horror stories about pornography, paedophilia, anarchism, bomb making and the rest have their roots in the newsgroups. But there are also civilised international chats about gardening, cycling and railway engines. Worth investigating, perhaps by using an index such as www. deja.com/news to help you find relevant subjects.

O

Offline

Not connected to the Internet. If you are paying by the minute for Internet access it obviously pays to work offline whenever possible. You should write and read your email offline, but you can also download long web pages to read at your leisure. Go to the File menu in your browser and then select 'Work Offline' (Internet Explorer) or 'Offline' followed by 'Work Offline'.

Online

Connected to the Internet, either at this moment or in general.

Online Services

Before the Internet really took off, there were a host of

Online Services, offering a private, closed network of users and a vast array of 'content'. Mostly they have disappeared as users have opted to take their chances with the whole Internet. But AOL and CompuServe have survived, both offering access to the Internet on top of their own membership world. For those who are nervous of the Internet, they offer a gentle introduction. Both are constantly offering free trials. CompuServe these days considers itself a business service, offering local access in most countries in the world. AOL is more family-directed. If you require the specific content they offer, including databases, news feeds, magazines and expert advice, they may be worth it, but most people find that they rapidly pass through the membership area to the Internet itself, which can be found cheaper and more efficiently elsewhere. Information from **www.aol.com** or **www.compuserve. com**. Or by telephone: AOL 0800 2791234; CompuServe 0990 134819.

P

Password
Basic security device used to ensure that you, and only you, can gain access to your computer, your ISP, your email account, your bank account and anything you sign up to on the web. Good passwords include a combination of letters and figures and don't make real words: unfortunately, they are impossible to remember. The proliferation of passwords and PIN numbers in people's lives means most revert to insecure practices, such as writing them down. Most 'hacking' is actually the result of people surreptitiously obtaining passwords.

Platform
A piece of jargon meaning the computer or other device from which you access the Internet, or the particular operating system software you are using. The PC and the Macintosh OS are platforms; so are WAP (Wireless Access

Protocol) phones and the set-top box used by television viewers to access the web.

Plug-in

An extra piece of software that is added to a main program, for instance a browser, to enable it to do a special job. If your browser comes across a file that needs a plug-in, it will alert you and show you how to download it. Otherwise, go to Plug-In Plaza (**http://browserwatch. internet.com/plug-in.html** to collect the set. Sites requiring a lot of specialised plug-ins are unpopular with ordinary web users.

POP

Acronym standing for two separate things: Point Of Presence and Post Office Protocol. A point of presence is the number your ISP gives you to dial in to. A big ISP will have lots all over the world. Post Office Protocol (also known as POP3) is the system most people use when they collect email from their mailboxes. Users of POP3 can also read their mail from a web page, but it remains on the server, which is handy if you are travelling. See **www. emailaddresses.com** for options.

Porn

Yes, the Internet is full of it. It is said that 40 per cent of all Internet searches are by people looking for pornographic material, and that 70 per cent of the web's entire capacity for data transfer is taken up by pornographic images: this is because they are very large files. While the rest of the e-commerce world wonders when it will make a profit, porn sites are supposedly set to make $2 billion this year (2000). They make their money by luring potential customers to look at free pictures in the hope that they will be persuaded to sign up for paid-for material. Because fewer than a thousand curious viewers of the free stuff actually jump that barrier, adverts for the free pictures are spread very widely indeed. Many of the large search-engine companies carry those advertising banners, triggered by the appropriate key words.

If you want to find porn, you already know where to look. If you don't want to find it, ensure you click on the 'family' or 'adult content' filters on any search engines you use, to avoid getting it by accident. There are filters built into your browser that you can activate, or you can use 'nannying' software. If you are worried about your children, sit with them while they search the Internet.

Portal
Any website intended to be a popular entrance point to the Internet. It hopes to use that passing traffic to generate advertising income.

Post
To send messages to a newsgroup to be read by all its readers.

Privacy
How much privacy can you expect when you use the Internet? The short answer is none. When your computer (the client) asks another computer (the server) for a web page, it sends an identifying number known as its IP address. It also sends details of the web page you want, and the web page you have just come from. It tells the server its operating system and the browser it is using. Your computer may hand over your email address, and if you have registered at a particular site it will also send those personal details. All these things are stored on the server for an indefinite time. So someone out there knows what you have been doing, if they can be bothered to look. This is one reason why you need to trust your ISP.

In practice, if you are dialling up from home, your IP number will change every time you use your ISP. But your ISP will have records of who used what ISP at what time, and these can be surrendered if there's a court order. So be aware that if you do anything illegal on the Net, you can be found out. This is even without the government's proposed new powers to place a device in each ISP so that the Home Secretary knows what everyone is doing on the Internet.

Then there are cookies (see above). When you go to a site, it sends you a 'cookie'. When you go back, the site asks for it, and that way knows you have been before. The page may greet you by name, but it has access only to information you have given it. However, cookies can be used to track your path around the web, and companies are increasingly tying those to your personal details to create a profile they can sell to marketing interests. Information from Cookie Central (**www.cookiecentral.com**).

Meanwhile, your own computer always stores (in your browser's History file and Cache) exactly what you have been looking at and when. Anyone who can get into your machine can look at your email. Anyone who can get into your correspondents' machines can look at the email you have sent them. Email gives the illusion of being private correspondence. In practice, it is anything but. In any case, people habitually copy and forward email to other people without asking permission.

Contributions to mailing lists and Usenet groups are almost invariably archived. Check on the policy of any list if this worries you. All of which means that any use of the Internet means leaving a trail. Check by searching for yourself in a few search engines.

Those who are worried about this can take two paths. The first is anonymity. You need not use your real name in your email and newsgroups, although many people consider it good manners. Hotmail will supply you as many aliases as you like: but they can be traced back to you in sufficiently serious circumstances. You can also use an anonymous remailer service. Details from Anonymizer. com (**www.anonymizer.com**), which covers privacy in detail. It also has a system to allow you to use the web without sites knowing anything about you.

Another strategy for privacy is encryption: encoding

your material so that it can't be read by anyone without your co-operation. The use of a program like PGP (Pretty Good Privacy) works for material in transit or on your hard disk. Details and downloads from The International PGP Home Page (**www.pgpi.org**).

The best approach, perhaps, is never to do or say anything on the Internet that you wouldn't own up to on your own doorstep.

Q

QuickTime

System invented by Apple for compressing video, sounds and pictures so they can be sent over the Internet. QuickTime files are played back using a plug-in for your browser or a program called the QuickTime Player. These are free and widely distributed. If you want to create QuickTime files, you have to pay.

R

RealAudio

RealAudio is a system for sending 'streaming' audio over the Net. This means sound that starts playing even before the whole file has arrived at your computer. To play RealAudio files you need a program called RealPlayer or a plug-in for your browser, available from Real.com (**www.realaudio.com**). Note: you cannot save RealAudio sounds. If you click on the file to play them again, your browser will start to reopen the connection so it can download the sounds all over again.

RealVideo

RealVideo is the video equivalent of RealAudio. It allows 'streaming' video over the net. But if you are limited to normal telephone-line access, video over the Internet is of novelty value only.

S

Search agent

A program you keep on your computer to help you find things by querying numerous search engines and sorting out the best results. The most advanced is probably Copernic (**www.copernic.com**), a basic version of which is available free. For Macs, Sherlock comes built in, but it needs to be kept up to date with new plug-ins from **www. apple.com/sherlock**. Windows users might like to try Kanjen, an ingenious new program from **www.autonomy. com** that summarises documents on your screen and uses that as the basis of its search.

Search engine

A website that helps you find things by 'full-text searching'. You type in a word, or words, and it looks to see if it can find them in the sites it has catalogued. Even the most powerful of the search engines catalogues only a proportion of the Internet. Nonetheless, basic queries can yield thousands of responses. Each search engine has its own rules about how you should phrase your enquiries. Look for a help link and download the instructions. Search engines are good for finding very specific things. They are less good at finding a range of similar things: for that you would normally use a directory. Try Google (**www.google. co.uk**), AltaVista (**www.altavista.com**) or FAST (**www. alltheweb.com**). Detailed information about search engines and how to use them can be found at Search Engine Watch (**www.searchenginewatch.com**).

Security

Security means stopping other people looking at your documents and interfering with them. It is primarily a problem for people running servers, the big computers that hold websites and databases. That obviously affects you when your information is held there. What's more, people may be able to get into your computer. And finally there is the problem of whether the connections between you and the server are secure.

Modern browsers attempt to deal with some of these problems. When you see a web address that begins 'https://' you are dealing with a 'secure' site. Anything you type in – a credit-card number, for instance – will be encoded before it is sent and decoded at the server end. You know you are at a 'secure' site because a closed padlock icon will appear at the bottom of your browser screen. Credit-card fraud certainly exists on the Internet, but then it does in restaurants and shops.

Unfortunately, most of the recent techniques used to create 'active content' in web pages (animation, games, personalised content) also have the potential to make a hole in your computer's defences. In Preferences, find 'Security' or 'Security zones' and you will see that your browser can be adjusted to warn you when you are about to download something potentially damaging or enter an insecure site. Most people leave this alone, but those who are very worried will switch off Java, ActiveX and cookies and set a 'High' security zone.

Viruses enter by the routes that information leaks out. Even something as apparently harmless as a Microsoft Word or Excel file can contain a virus in its associated 'macros'. Everyone who uses the Internet should have some kind of antivirus software and keep it up to date.

Server
A large computer used to store documents, programs, websites, email and so on. In the 'client–server' relationship, your computer is the 'client'.

Shareware
This is software made available for download and distribution on the basis that you will pay for it after trying it. Some shareware continues to function whether or not you register and pay for it. Some works but won't let you save what you are doing. Some stops working altogether after a period of time. Shareware is not to be confused with

freeware, which is free but must not be rewritten, and public-domain (or PD) software, which is free and can be modified as much as you like. Good shareware is often comparable to commercial products, and well worth paying for.

Shockwave
A system that uses a plug-in program, available from Macromedia (**www.macromedia.com**), to display effects, games and animations on web pages.

Shopping
You can now buy just about anything on the web. The pioneers of online shopping thought retailers would cluster together in 'online malls', but it has not worked out like that. Online shops attract customers just as real ones do – by advertising. So you will see most of the big outlets pushing their web addresses hard on poster sites and television. You have a choice between online-only shops and those that also have a high street presence – the so-called 'clicks and mortar' sector.

You can find the web addresses of most of the prominent shops by using a directory such as Yahoo! or Excite. Failing that, there are numerous specialised directory sites of shops. Try **www.i-stores.co.uk** or **www.shopsmart.com** or **www.shopandsave.com**. There seems little real point to any of them.

More useful are the shopping agents: sites and small programs that look for a product and find you the best possible price. The best examples are American: see My Simon (**www.mysimon.com**) to see how it should be done. But British examples are arriving all the time. Try Checkaprice UK (**www.checkaprice.co.uk**) or Pricewatch UK (**www.pricewatch.co.uk**), which specialises in computers. For books there is Book Brain (**www.bookbrain.co.uk**), which tells you how much each online bookshop charges to deliver and how long it takes: very revealing. The American giant Bottom Dollar (**www.bottomdollar.com**)

now includes a few British shops, but don't expect them to sell things at anywhere near the American price.

Smiley

Also known as an emoticon, a smiley is the happy face made with a colon and a closing bracket, like this: :) Turn your head on one side and you may see it. From that tiny acorn has grown a whole world of faces made out of punctuation. Amusing, but hardly used in real life. There's a comprehensive list at **www.netlingo.com/smiley**. This one, by the way, is Marge Simpson: @@@@:-)

Spam

Junk email or advertisements sent to lots of different newsgroups indiscriminately. If you don't like your mailbox being filled up with circulars from get-rich-quick scams and Russian dating agencies, you can take certain preventive actions. Spammers work by 'harvesting' email addresses from newsgroups and other public areas, as well as buying them from organisations you have signed up to in good faith. If you don't want to be harvested, get a free email account from Hotmail or similar and use a false name when you are contributing to these public areas. That way all the junk mail goes to Hotmail and you needn't bother about it. Your 'real' email remains open for real correspondence.

You can also complain to the 'domain' that the spam is coming from. If the trouble comes from **spamster@spam. com** a message to **postmaster@spam.com** should reach the person responsible for ensuring the site complies with law and good practice. But few spammers use their real email addresses. Never reply to any piece of spam, even those inviting you to 'ask to be taken off our mailing list'. That simply proves to the spammer that your address is real, and you will get lots more.

There are various utilities that allow you to delete spam before you download it: search TUCOWS (**www.tucows. com**) or similar under 'anti-spam'. And modern email programs allow you to filter email as it reaches your computer.

One filter that is often used is to tell the program to remove any messages that don't have your actual email address in their 'To:' field. Spam often arrives like this, because it has been sent as a 'blind carbon copy' of a message nominally sent to someone else. That way the spammer keeps his list of victims to himself.

There are more drastic methods. One is to change your email address in some obvious way so that human beings have to manually adjust it before they respond to you. For instance, you might change your email to **johnDELETE-CAPS-TO-REPLY@smallprovider.com**, perhaps telling people in your 'signature' to do exactly that. But doing that may seriously inconvenience anyone who wants to write to you for legitimate reasons. Unless you are the victim of a massive spam 'attack', you may choose just to ignore it. Usually it is no worse than having a lot of pizza-delivery fliers pushed through your door.

There are comprehensive notes on the problem and possible solutions at **http://spam.abuse.net**. A simpler approach – though with a more complicated address – is to be found at **www.pwrtc.com/~wdegroot/spam.html**.

Streaming

System that allows you to view or hear video or sound without having to download the whole file first. Used by RealAudio and RealVideo and QuickTime plug-ins.

Subscribe

To choose some out of the 30,000 or so Usenet newsgroups offered by the average ISP so that they are immediately available. First load the whole list – it will take a while – then highlight the ones you want and select 'Subscribe'.

You can also subscribe to a mailing list. Most are automated, and require no more from you than an email with the word 'subscribe' in either the 'body' or the 'subject' panel.

In Internet Explorer, you can also subscribe to web pages. This places them in your Favorites list and checks them at regular intervals to see whether they have been changed. A little icon appears beside the page's name to tell you whether it has anything new.

None of these subscriptions involve paying out any money, although there are paid-for mailing lists and publications if you want them.

T

TCP/IP

TCP/IP is the software that makes the Internet work. IP (Internet Protocol) gives everything on the Internet an address and moves information around. TCP (Transmission Control Protocol) packages up information from the individual programs on your computer to send across the wire. It also unpacks any incoming information, and ensures that transmissions get through, sending them again if necessary.

The best advice about all this is to ignore it. If your Internet connection is working, leave it alone. If you must fiddle with it, perhaps because your ISP has told you to, make sure you write down any information you see in the appropriate control panels before you start changing things. That way you will (probably) be able to put it back.

Finding TCP/IP information on the Mac is easy: there's a control panel called precisely that. In Windows, take a deep breath and burrow down the following path: Start Menu/ Settings/Control Panel/Internet Options/Connections. Then highlight your ISP's name and start burrowing again: Settings/Properties/Server Types. Then click the button saying 'TCP/IP settings'.

Realistically, the only thing you can do with TCP/IP is to ensure you have a valid DNS address. Check it with your ISP if you are having trouble connecting to web pages. In the Mac, go to the TCP/IP panel and type a new number into the box called 'Name Server addr:'. In

Windows you may be using a DNS address assigned to you by the server, and if that works leave it alone. If not, click the button marked 'Specify name server addresses' and type the address into the spaces. It will have four numbers between 0 and 255, separated by dots.

Thread

A single continuous discussion in a newsgroup or a series of messages on the same subject. Your mail program will offer you the option of sorting your inbox messages 'by thread' (in Netscape) or 'threading' them (in Internet Explorer), which means grouping them by subject.

Newsreader programs and mail programs will group newsgroup contributions by thread, meaning by subject. Then, when you respond, you can add to the thread, start a new thread (by typing a new subject into the 'subject' box), or write back to an individual author by private email.

Trojan Horse

A Trojan Horse (often called just a Trojan) is a virus that disguises itself as something useful or entertaining, so that you double-click the file to start it up. Then it eats your hard disk. Never open any attached file, particularly any .exe file, if you don't know what it is or who it is from.

U

Upload

To send material from your computer to a central server, for instance to update your own web page. You can do it with Netscape but not Internet Explorer. You may be better off using a proper FTP program.

URL

Universal Resource Locator, meaning the address of a page or file somewhere on the Internet. The first bit, up to the double-slash, tells you what type of thing is to be found at that address: http:// is a web page, ftp:// is a file that has to be downloaded to your computer. The next section, from the double-slash to the first single slash, tells you the host and domain where the material is kept: **somewhere.co.uk**. Anything after that first single slash tells you where the file is kept within the host computer system. If the URL ends in a series of letters and numbers with a dot in the middle, that's a file. The letters after the dot indicates the type of file.

So **http://www.whotnot.co.uk/homepage/images/mugshot.gif** means a 'gif' picture file called mugshot, in a directory or folder called images, inside another directory called homepage, on a host computer belonging to a company called whotnot, that can be reached with a web browser. If you can't get through, try removing the bits between the slash marks one at a time, starting at the end.

Usenet

Usenet, which is short for Users' Network, is the worldwide discussion area made up of thousands of 'newsgroups'. Usenet and newsgroups are used interchangeably. The newsgroups are organised in groups by subject matter: news; comp (computers); alt (alternative: just about anything); misc. (miscellaneous); biz (business and marketing); rec (recreation); talk (debate); soc (society); and sci (science). Within those are various categories and subcategories, separated by dots, in the group's name: **alt.english.usage**, for instance, is an 'alternative' group about the use of English. To find groups, do a search on the 40,000-strong list downloaded by your mail or news program, or search in depth through a site such as **www.deja.com/news**. Usenet has no central administration, so groups make their own rules. More information from the Internet FAQ Archives (**www.faqs.org/faqs/usenet/**).

V

Video

It is perfectly possible for video pictures to travel across the Internet to be shown on your computer. Your browser will need a plug-in to suit the type of video file being sent. The leading plug-ins are the RealPlayer from Real Networks (**www.real.com**) and Apple's QuickTime player (**www.apple.com/quicktime**). There are also competing systems for sending video pictures backwards and forwards in a videophone arrangement. No video system using normal telephone access has yet produced anything other than a tiny and unreliable picture. When 'broadband' Internet becomes available, then Internet video will stop being a mere novelty and become a real rival to television.

Virus

A virus is a computer program designed to enter other people's systems illicitly and alter the way they work. It may damage or wipe files, prevent the system working properly or just display irritating messages from the moron who created it. It spreads because it attaches itself to files that human beings then send around the world on floppy disks or across the Internet.

Viruses infect programs and parts of your computer's system software. They don't normally infect documents (word processor files, pictures, emails, etc.) but they can infect documents that include 'macros', little programs designed to help you work. They are typically passed on through 'attachments' sent along with email.

Viruses are inactive until you launch the infected program or open the infected document. Then they lodge themselves in the computer, doing what damage they can, and wait for someone to pass them on.

Two specialised types of virus are Trojan Horses (or Trojans) and worms. Trojan Horses look as if they are doing something useful or amusing, but behind that they are creating havoc. Worms seek out specific files on your hard disk and try to destroy them. More importantly, they are designed to spread themselves without your doing anything. They simply make email programs send them to everyone in their address book.

One popular preventive strategy is this: never open an attachment sent by someone you don't know. If you download shareware and freeware, place it in a separate folder and run your antivirus program over it before you open it. Keep your antivirus program up to date: they need to be updated to help prevent new strains. And the browser makers are constantly producing 'patches' to counter the security threats their programs persist in letting in. You can download them for nothing, and you should. Detailed information, albeit rather self-interested, from the makers of the antivirus programs: Symantec (**www.symantec.com**) and McAfee (**www.mcafee.com**). A good starting point for beginners might be **www.faqs.org/faqs/computer-virus/new-users/**.

Most importantly, you should back up all your important material by copying it to some other medium: usually a Zip disk or a series of floppies.

W

WAP
Wireless Access Protocol. The new standard for mobile phones that allows them to access the Internet. Unfortunately, the average mobile phone screen can display no more than about fifteen words, meaning that they can use only special cut-down web pages and not the real thing.

warez
Slang term meaning software, usually pirated. Used in the titles of various newsgroups.

wav
A type of sound file for Windows, using the suffix '.wav' and known as 'wave'.

Web page
A document made up of words, graphics, photographs and sometimes video and sounds, designed to be sent over the Internet and looked at on a screen.

Web site
A group of linked web pages created by a person or organisation.

Webmaster
Person responsible for building and maintaining a website. Not to be confused with postmaster, a person responsible for maintaining an Internet domain.

World Wide Web
Millions of documents stored as web pages on the world's computers and made accessible through the Internet. The World Wide Web is administered by the World Wide Web Consortium, which is often known as W3C. Its website is unfortunately rather intimidating, though full of useful information: **www.w3c.org**. It is curious that in such a fast-moving world, the definitive account of all things to do with the web, the World Wide Web FAQ, actually dates back to 1994. Get it from **www.boutell.com/faq/ oldfaq/wwwfaq.txt**, along with various newer versions.

WYSIWYG
Stands for 'what you see is what you get', and it means just that. For instance, a typical document you prepare using a word processor will these days look much as it will look when you've printed it out (in Word's Page View mode, for instance), whereas with earlier word processors you needed to go to a special preview screen.

Z

Zip

Two distinct meanings:

- the trade name of a type of removable disk drive, used for storing and transporting files.
- a system for compressing files so they use less space on a disk and take less time to send across the Internet. Zipped files, which have the suffixes .zip, .gz and .tgz, must be expanded before they can be used.

On Windows you need a program such as Winzip (**www.winzip.com**), which will cost $29, or Aladdin Expander (**www.aladdinsys.com**), which is free. On the Mac, use Stuffit Expander (**www.aladdinsys.com**), which came with your computer, or is a free download.

6 Sites for Sore Eyes

Here are a few sites designed to introduce you to the Internet experience. Rather than putting in lots of identical online shops or magazines or encyclopedias, I have tried to find examples that do something that only the Internet can give you. That means I have consistently chosen interesting ideas rather than polished presentation.

Where possible, I have gone for sites with strong British content, but sadly, where a lot of sites are offering the same type of thing, the British version is rarely the best. Too many of our sites are pale imitations of things done better elsewhere, and you don't want to waste your time with those when you can see the real thing. It is particularly disappointing that few British sites have come up with new ideas for using the technology. Of course, the best sites for you will be the ones you find yourself. Don't forget to recommend them to others.

INTERNET TOOLS AND HELPERS

Yahoo! UK & Ireland (www.yahoo.co.uk)

I make no apologies for starting with the tools you will need to use the Internet, beginning with perhaps the most famous brand name of them all. This is a slightly cut-down version of the American Yahoo! site, offering a huge range of facilities as well as the basic directory function. If you do want to have a home page specified in your Browser, this is as good as any, and certainly better than the one your ISP will provide.

To use a directory like this, you can either click on the

big headings in the centre of the page ('Arts & Humanities', 'News & Media' and so on), or go to the selection of subheadings shown here ('Literature', 'Photography' . . .), or you can use the search box. Start by doing it through the category headings. Say you want to find out anything you can about Pembrokeshire, because you're going there for a holiday. Look under 'Recreation & Sport' and you will find 'Travel'. Click that, and you're on a page full of travel links. Click 'UK Only', and you go to a page just of UK travel links: no information as yet. England is here, and Scotland, but no Wales.

Never mind, try 'Destination Guides'. Another page of links, arranged alphabetically as always. But here you find 'Wales Accommodation Guide and Tourist Information' and 'Welcome To Wales'. Click either of those to be taken to the actual sites. Well, Welcome To Wales seems not to include anything south of Brecon. And Wales Accommodation Guide, etc. is mainly that.

Perhaps we'd have fared better by using the search box on the opening page. Click 'UK only' below the box and type something in. Try 'Pembrokeshire' and see what happens. Yahoo! searches its own headings first, and then the headings of the sites it lists. So your search reveals that there is a Pembrokeshire category in Yahoo!, which proves to be full of links to all manner of interesting stuff. We obviously started in the wrong place.

It also finds twenty sites with 'Pembrokeshire' in the title, leading us to cottages, sailing clubs and so on. If that had failed, we could have clicked a button to go to 'the whole of Yahoo', but that wouldn't have helped. We could also click a button marked 'Web Pages', at the top of any of these pages of links, and that would have sent us into the web itself: bringing in more than five thousand pages. But, if we were going to search the web, we should have been more precise.

Using search directories is a tricky business: they tend to give you very little until you persuade them to cough up more by opening up your search. This is the opposite to what happens with search engines, which give you everything at once and require you to ask for less.

But web search is now only a part of what a major 'portal' like Yahoo! offers. Go back to the main page and you will see that you can set up a free email service; personalise Yahoo! to your own requirements and register for extra services; go straight to well-produced pages about money, sport, weather and television; and send personalised email greetings cards. You can go to search databases full of jobs, homes and cars. You can use online calendars, an address book and even what Yahoo! calls a 'briefcase', meaning a storage area for your material on Yahoo!'s servers. You can also download software to enable you to 'chat' with your friends or with fellow Yahoo! enthusiasts. There are pages of constantly updated news headlines that you can configure to your own tastes. And there's a big children's section, Yahooligans! And that's just a smattering of the material available on the UK version of Yahoo! There are more for other countries.

Yahoo! should not be your only way of finding things, but it does offer an awful lot of facilities on one site – more so if you use the US version (www.yahoo.com).

Google (www.google.com)

If you want a search engine, and you don't want all the other trimmings, you can't do better than Google. It has a clean front page with no unnecessary clutter or advertisements, it works well and, perhaps best of all, if it lists a page you know you are going to be able to see it because it holds copies of every page it ever points you to. The drawback is that it is American, rather than British, but if that is central to your search you can type 'UK' into the search box alongside the thing you are looking for.

Most search engines work in the same way, but Google has a big idea of its own, which is to rank the pages it finds for you according to how many other pages link to them. It's a kind of popularity contest for web pages, and it seems to work. It also has certain quirks in the way it asks you to write your queries.

Remember that to use a search engine you need to have a specific target in mind. Then you construct your search by putting a lot of words in the box so the search is narrowed down. Google helps here, because it brings up only pages that have all your search words in them. So if we type 'Pembrokeshire beach holiday attractions', we will get only pages including all those things. That brings up 211 pages, which is manageable. Some search engines would bring up pages containing *any* of those words, giving you several hundred thousand to wade through. Google lets you use phrasing, with speech marks, but it will not let you use 'wild cards', meaning asterisks. Its party trick is the 'I'm Feeling Lucky' button, which takes you to the site at the top of its lists. It's surprising how often this works. Google will also let you search sites in different languages, and it includes a fairly basic 'Safe Search' system to discourage your children from finding things that they shouldn't. No news, weather, email or flashing adverts, which can only be good. Oh, yes, if you prefer a search directory system, just click the 'browse by category' link and you'll be in Google's version of that. Or go straight to **http://directory.google.com**.

Jeeves (www.askjeeves.co.uk)

Jeeves may be the first character created by the Internet, especially now his creators have agreed terms with the PG Wodehouse estate. Jeeves enthusiasts like the way you can find things by typing your question into his box in your own language without worrying about 'searching' techniques. But how good is he? Ask him, 'What is there to do in Pembrokeshire?' and he finds a handful of items from commercial directories and organisations that have paid Jeeves for the privilege. Then there are his findings from search engines, which repeat themselves: Jeeves is obviously too busy butlering to remove the duplicates. Worth a look, because it is one of the most famous sites on the web and many people love it. But you might do better typing your question into one of the real search engines: it often works just as well as it does with Jeeves. In Google, for instance, it took me straight to 'Pembrokeshire-online What To Do'.

Dogpile (www.dogpile.com)
If you want to search lots of search engines at once rather than rely on just one, try Dogpile. It is fast and quite clever. It now also includes its own directory, as well as specialised searches for images and sounds and the usual portal features. Be aware that some of the things it finds will have paid for inclusion. If you want a clean screen, speed and no frills, try IxQuick (www.ixquick.com) or MetaEureka (www.metaeureka.com).

Mirago (www.mirago.co.uk)
If you want an interesting and quick UK-native search tool, try this one. It is rather idiosyncratic but can work well.

Deja (www.deja.com/usenet)
This is still the best tool for searching the Usenet newsgroups. Deja.com's front page is now devoted to shopping, but either take this direct route or click the link that says Search Discussions. Once you are there you can search recent and past discussions in Deja's huge archive. If you are keen you should click the Power Search link and learn to use those tools. Be warned: all sorts of activities are to be found in Usenet. You can reply to anything you read from here, without having to go back to your email program. A site called RemarQ (www.remarq.com) does a similar job.

ForumOne (www.forumone.com)
A site that allows you to search web forums, which are web-based versions of the Usenet newsgroups.

Liszt (www.liszt.com)

Go here to find out about 90,000 mailing lists. It doesn't actually offer much information about them, but it does automate the sign-up process. You might also look at www. egroups.com, which has just been absorbed by Yahoo!.

SearchEngineWatch (www.searchenginewatch.com)

Everything you ever wanted to know about how search engines and directories work. An excellent resource for anyone who wants to *use* the Internet rather than merely gawp at it.

Web100 (www.web100.com)

Sometimes you just want to look at things other people recommend. Try Web100, where sites are supposedly reviewed by readers and placed in a Top 100 chart. Or try 100hot (www.100hot.com), which says what people are actually looking at. You will look hard for anything British in either list. The BBC's giant site does best, coming in at number 47 in 100hot.

Plug-in Plaza (www.browserwatch.internet.com/plug-in.html)

Sooner or later you will go to a site that won't work properly because you don't have the right 'plug-in' for your browser. If you are lucky you will be automatically redirected to this site, which will then steer you to wherever you have to be to do the necessary download. Most likely you will want something from the MultiMedia section. Take a note of what the onscreen message tells you when you run into plug-in trouble, then find a reference to the plug-in concerned in the Plug-in Plaza site. Then click where it says 'Sample Page' or 'Developer's URL' to discover how to proceed.

Macromedia (www.macromedia.com)

This is where you learn about two of the web's most ubiquitous brands of content, Shockwave and Flash, and get the necessary plug-ins. You may not want animation on your screen, but sites increasingly assume you will and won't work otherwise.

Real (www.real.com)
The RealPlayer allows you to listen to 'streaming' radio and television on your computer, meaning it starts playing even before you have finished downloading the file. You can download free versions of the necessary plug-in, or you can pay for it for slightly better results and facilities.

QuickTime (www.apple.com/quicktime)
This is the audio and video technology invented by Apple, but also widely used on Windows computers. You may be asked for the QuickTime plug-in. It is free from here.

Windows MediaPlayer (www.microsoft.com/windows/mediaplayer)
If you have Windows on your computer, you will probably have Windows MediaPlayer to play radio, video and MP3s. If you have a Mac, you probably won't be using it yet. Either way, you can download or upgrade here. Some people find it works better than RealPlayer, and sites are increasingly offering it instead.

Internet Explorer home page (www.microsoft.com/windows/Ie/Support/default.asp)
Everything you need to get Internet Explorer running properly and with luck keep it that way. Microsoft's Internet support system is sadly chaotic.

Netscape (http://help.netscape.com/products/client/communicator)
A page of links leading to lots of information about Netscape. Not as flashy as Microsoft's, but it is all there somewhere.

ZDNet Help & How-To (www.zdnet.com/zdhelp)
There is no shortage of sites for people seeking help with the Internet and computers generally, but this one, from the hi-tech publisher ZD, takes you all the way from

beginner to expert. The step-by-step how-tos are particularly useful.

Hotsheet (www.hotsheet.com)

A simple one-page list of all the most useful links. Indispensable but solidly American.

HEALTH AND LIFESTYLE

NetDoctor (www.netdoctor.co.uk)

There is no shortage of medical sites on the web, but this one is by far the best of the British examples. Indeed, it is one of the best British sites in any field, not least because of its clear, elegant design. Put together by a group of media doctors with solid backing, it steers clear of any ego trips and concentrates instead on providing both breadth and depth in its medical information. At the top of the page, where it should be, is the search box. Type in the condition or symptom you are interested in and it will take you straight to a bulging envelope full of notes on it, although a lot of these turn out to be duplicates. Nonetheless, it certainly handled my enquiries better than any of the rival British sites.

But that's a basic minimum for a medical site. This one sets out its other features with great clarity. There's an 'Encyclopedia', allowing you to look up diseases and conditions, medicines and health advice and collect factsheets on several broad topics including smoking, diabetes, children's health and vaccinations.

Then an 'Interactive' section takes you to medical news sources, lets you join an online discussion where site users share their problems, or email a question to the site's panel of doctors, headed by the medical celebrity Dr Hilary Jones. No answer is guaranteed, however, and you must agree that the advice does not replace a real medical consultation – and that you won't sue. My favourite bit of the 'Interactive' section is the area devoted to online tests, which assess your risk of diabetes or heart disease and your susceptibility to depression, among other things. You can even discover what day of the week you were born on, presumably to establish whether you are doomed to be full of woe for ever.

There's lots more, including occasional live 'chat', feature articles of various sorts and a search box for the exhaustive American medical database Medline. If all that's not enough you can sign up for a daily email newsletter containing the latest medical news.

Confetti (www.confetti.com)

Often the best website ideas are those with a narrow focus but real depth. Confetti comes into that category. It is all about weddings: planning them, organising them, paying for them and surviving them.

Underneath the calm exterior, in two shades of mauve, there is a solid focus on shopping, of course, but before you get down to ordering the wine and booking the honeymoon it offers useful advice and information for all parties involved in the happy day. There are different links depending upon your role, from bride and groom to page boy and flower girl. Topics such as speech making and music are well covered, with a lot of funny anecdotes to keep you in a light-hearted mood despite the onset of pre-matrimonial tension.

For those wishing to step outside the traditional norm, humanist ceremonies and 'themed' weddings are also featured.

When you get to the shopping area, things are nicely presented on the page, and you get the choice of buying them as a gift or adding them to your wedding list. Thereafter it is the normal online shopping pattern: a shopping basket, registration and secure payment. But most of the goods come not from Confetti but from its 'retail partners', which means that there is no common price or timing for deliveries. Some take up to a month to deliver, and under 'returns policy' one simply states: 'Do not have one'. Presumably they are banking on no one sending back a wedding present.

Handbag.com (www.handbag.com)

An elegant pastel-coloured site that looks and reads like a mass-market women's magazine with an emphasis on good advice. Owned by Boots, which might have found leaflets a cheaper and more effective way of spreading the word. But still the least pretentious and irritating of the women's-interest sites.

Liv4now (www.liv4now.com)

Another lifestyle site, but this one is younger and apparently aimed at both sexes. It also has a strong emphasis on humour, with lots of the funny lists that you will soon discover are the main burden on the transatlantic email system. Read them all here first. Over-eighteens only.

Ready2Shop (www.ready2shop.com)

Who wants to look at fashion on the web? Not everyone, but you might try this British site, because it has a real sense of fun, from the opening 'splash page' onwards. It invites you to tell it about your body shape, and what you like or dislike about it, using a highly ambitious bit of programming that doesn't quite work. Then it bases its recommendations on that. You can email pictures of what it chooses to a friend.

Hairdos.com (www.hairdos.com)

Exactly what the address suggests. Tell this US site your desired hair colour, length and degree of curl and it will conjure up a page of assorted 'dos' for you to examine or print out and wave at your hairdresser. An amazing popular success despite its limitations.

About.com Healing (www.healing.about.com)

About.com is like a more polished version of Yahoo! and this is an excellent collection of links to US alternative-medicine sites. Untroubled by scepticism, or so my spirit guide tells me.

UK Parents (www.ukparents.co.uk)
Not the most sophisticated of sites to look at but full of interest and assistance for those bringing up children. Questions answered by a panel of doctors, health visitors and counsellors. A good home-grown effort.

PetPlanet (www.petplanet.co.uk)
Solid site for pet-lovers, with a built-in secure shopping site. It caters mainly for dog and cat lovers and has a few peculiarities, including different search boxes for different areas of the site. An alternative to the highly publicised www.pets-pyjamas.com, which has similar material but keeps it under the well-stocked counter.

The Longevity Game (http://northwesternmutual.com/games/longevity)
From a large US life-assurance company, try this interactive game and discover how long until you shuffle off. Observe how your life expectancy grows or shrinks as you answer questions about eating, drinking, height, weight and family history. Only on the web can you do things like this.

Quiz Box Tests (www.quizbox.com)
A whole battery of personality tests, love tests, compatibility tests, quizzes and puzzles offering instant results and analysis. Strictly for fun.

HOME AND GARDEN

Expert Gardener (www.expertgardener.com)
Gardening and computers would not seem to be an obvious combination, but there are lots of high-profile sites for those with green fingers – or hoping to acquire them. If you don't have violent objections to Alan Titchmarsh and Charlie Dimmock, try Expert Gardener.

Many of the gardening sites are really aimed at beginners,

reluctant pruners and those whose idea of gardening is going to visit one, preferably with a teashop. Others, notably **www.greenfingers.com**, are basically online garden centres and gadget shops with a bit of advice attached. But Expert Gardener presents itself as a gardening club, with a strong emphasis on its 'communities', meaning discussion areas. It is bright and well presented, with the usual animations as you run your mouse over the menu items. As mentioned, the television gardening duo are prominently featured, with a chatty newsletter from Titchmarsh if you register. Registration itself is straightforward and asks no intrusive questions.

Inside the site you will find constantly updated gardening headlines, searches of the site itself and a database of public gardens, a monthly magazine that is not remotely intimidating, a three-day weather forecast for your region and a couple of bits that aren't finished: these include the shop, which means a refreshing lack of hard-sell but may deter some. One amusing feature is the animated 3D garden planner. The creators of this site are expert enough to admit that this is really a bit of fun. If you like that kind of thing, try the BBC's The Garden (**www.bbc.co.uk/thegarden**) but be warned that you must register and spend ten minutes downloading a peculiar plug-in.

Expert Gardener is a strangely offputting title for what is actually a very approachable page. In particular, you will enjoy the discussions, where gardeners rally round to assist one another, like a more democratic version of Gardeners' Question Time.

diyfixit (www.diyfixit.co.uk)

There are plenty of impressively designed American DIY sites, but what use are they for those of us who live in a country that doesn't even know whether we're metric or imperial? This site doesn't look as stylish as some – unless you like little Flash-animated puppets – but it is full of information about basic DIY jobs, from fixing loose floorboards to rehanging a door. You can find information by nominating the room you are considering or by the type of job – electrics, tiling, plumbing and so on. Whichever way you do it, the same information comes up. The instruction sheets are clear, and are accompanied by simple step-by-step diagrams. It's a bit like the old *Reader's Digest* DIY manual, but free and a lot less ambitious.

The emphasis is on bashing wood and slapping paint rather than consulting colour swatches and distributing objets – old-fashioned home improvements rather than design. At the same time, it is not the place to look if you are planning a loft conversion, but it does have a link to Homepro.com (**www.homepro.com**), an agency for professional building tradesmen. And there you can also find information on more ambitious projects, including advice on planning permission and building regulations. Diyfixit has no shop, surviving on the ads it carries from people like Evo-Stik. Those wanting a more commercial, design-orientated emphasis should look at **www.diy.co.uk**, which is owned by B&Q, or **www.homebase.co.uk**. But it is hard to find this sort of simple practical guidance in either.

Homes By Design (www.homesbydesign.co.uk)
This site is sponsored by Dulux. If you don't mind that, it offers a lot of advice and information about colour combinations and how much wallpaper to buy.

Learn2.com (www.learn2.com/browse/all_2torials.asp)
Typing in this tricky address will take you straight to the complete list of this American site's excellent '2torials'. Choose 'Home & Garden', where it says 'Select A Channel', and then soak up everything from 'Build a window box' to 'Prepare for an earthquake', with a lot of straightforward domestic stuff in between. Brilliantly done.

Fish4homes (www.fish4homes.co.uk)

Interested in buying a house online? There are plenty of sites packed with useful information about the process, the finances and the legalities. There are also lots of online property databases. But the biggest and most straightforward is probably this one, using the resources of Britain's local newspapers. Worth trying, but don't expect to be overwhelmed by numbers: Internet property sales are still rare.

ihavemoved (www.ihavemoved.com)

On the web the simplest ideas are often the best. This site takes details of your old address and your new one and then informs all the relevant utilities and service companies. And all for nothing: the site pays for itself by taking a fee from the companies you notify.

UpMyStreet (www.upmystreet.com)

One of the few British sites that show a spark of real innovation, this allows you to type in your postcode or town name (or any others, for that matter) so that you can discover local property prices, crime rates, schools and their performance, council statistics and local facilities. All are presented as graphs, where possible, letting you see your house price soar or slump. Irresistible. But the site is underpowered and slow, so you may have to be patient.

BBC Antiques (www.bbc.co.uk/antiques)

Probably the most stylish and approachable of all the online antiques sites, this is a typically thorough and sensible BBC product. Go to the Message Board and marvel at the stuff some people turn up. Then check the database of *Antiques Roadshow* 'finds' to see what it may be worth.

OrganizedHome.com (http://organizedhome.com)

Terrifying but impressive American site full of ideas on how to 'organize/declutter/simplify/clean' your home. Includes several complex systems for achieving simplicity.

Food and Drink (www.bbc.co.uk/foodanddrink)
There are lots of vast American recipe and cookery sites,
but how many people in Britain want to eat like that? The
BBC's show gains a lot in its Internet version: you get all
the ingredients in proper measurements, all the instructions, and you can't hear the presenters.

Wine Spectator (www.winespectator.com)
The biggest and most impressive wine site on the web.
Search its cellar for an instant percentage score on any
wine tasted in the last couple of years. Rich, well-
structured with a glossy finish.

SHOPPING

Valuemad (www.valuemad.com)
The real point of Internet shopping is price. No one does it
because they want to feel the quality of the merchandise.
Checking the price of an item at lots of places at once is
something you can do only on the web, which is why
'price comparison' or 'shopping agent' sites such as Valuemad are often busy.

Once you get in, however, the site is straightforward
enough to navigate, although the designer is slightly in
love with the idea of 'shopping bots'. These clever bits of
software are here turned into lovable animated figures
who wobble around the site while you wait for it to do its
searches. Those who dislike such fripperies should head
straight for Checkaprice (**www.checkaprice.co.uk**), which
does the same job with an uglier interface. Valuemad
seems to offer more areas to compare, however: audio-
visual, books, computers, financial services, flowers,
kitchen appliances, music, videos, phones and travel, with
bikes and cameras promised.

First you tell it that you want to search by price, then
you select the category, then you fill in a few details about
the product you are looking for. Wait, while watching an

animated robot push a supermarket trolley, and the comparisons appear. Price includes VAT and delivery for most items, and the site makes an effort to provide a delivery time, so you can be sure when you are comparing like with like. The results can be remarkable. A span from £10.95 to £18.02 for the same CD, for instance.

The site also offers information on the products it sells, taken from a large database of online reviews, and a changing selection of 'hot deals'. When you decide whom you want to buy from, you click on an icon and are taken to that retailer's site: Valuemad has done its bit, although it will try to gather your email address as you pass through. When you get there, you find that the retailer has already placed your item in its shopping cart. But don't be intimidated by this haste: you haven't bought anything until you type in your card number.

A good start for British comparison shopping, but take a look at US sites like Bottom Dollar (**www.bottomdollar. com**) to see how it *can* be done – and Bottom Dollar has now started to list some British prices.

eBay (www.ebay.co.uk)

Comparison searches are one of the ways the Internet has changed shopping. The other is the online auction. The American site eBay is one of the most successful of all Internet businesses, because it makes it easy for people to spend money. Now it has brought its formula to Britain, where it offers local web users the opportunity to bid for items in the UK or abroad. On the left of its start page it has a list of categories, Yahoo! style, or you can use a search box to go straight to the things you are interested in.

A search on 'guitar', for instance, takes you to a list of current auctions that, when I checked it out, contained everything from a Paul McCartney promotional plectrum to a boxed Elvis Presley toy guitar of the 1950s. Clicking on the item brings up a page that tells you how long the auction has to run, what the current highest bid stands at, how many bids there have been, the currency the auction is taking place in and so on.

There is also usually a picture of the item and some history, and a panel telling you how to bid. To do that you must register, and then you can place a maximum bid, beyond which you will not go. Obviously that is secret from other bidders. You are warned that the bid constitutes a contract: if you win, you will be expected to pay up. You make arrangements for payment and carriage between yourselves. Before you bid you can check the seller's record and reputation with other eBay members, and, if you are robbed, eBay will compensate you: up to £120 minus £15 deductions, although that won't get you very far if you're buying an Elvis Presley toy guitar.

BookBrain (www.bookbrain.co.uk)
Sometimes specialist price-comparison sites do a better job than the department-store version. Certainly if you are looking for a book it's better to go straight to BookBrain than wait for Valuemad's robots to do their stuff.

Computer Prices UK (www.computerprices.co.uk)
Fast and reliable price-comparison site for computer hardware and peripherals. Information on the products is available, and clicking on 'Buy Now' takes you straight to the dealer's shopping area.

letsbuyit.com (www.letsbuyit.com)
Another highly publicised new shopping idea. This time you club together with others to try to force down the price of an item. Search by category or keyword and check out the 'best price' possible if enough people join a sale. Make sure you actually get a bargain, though.

CDNOW (www.cdnow.co.uk)
An online record shop. Nothing very exciting there, perhaps, except that you can listen to the songs before you buy, in either RealAudio or MPEG form. RealAudio uses our RealPlayer plug-in, whereas the MPEG samples will

call up Windows Media Player or QuickTime player. A painless way of broadening your tastes.

Carbusters.com (www.carbusters.com)

Attempt by the Consumers' Association to solve the 'Great British car rip-off' by helping consumers buy from abroad. A very slick operation, but don't expect to be driving one of these cars by the weekend. Some have very long delivery dates indeed, so be sure you are getting a bargain.

Autotrader (www.autotrader.co.uk)

The online version of the used-car bible, which also features masses of information on new vehicles. Find the new car you like and it will quote you a price and arrange for a local dealer to call you. The used-car section, meanwhile, is not unlike the print version to look at, except that you don't have to leaf through hundreds of Mondeos to find the Fiat Barchetta your heart desires. You use an onscreen form and go straight to it. The site will also help direct you to finance and insurance.

Sainsbury's (www.sainsburys.co.uk)

Do you really want to do your supermarket shopping online? Well, you can, but it's a slow process, at least the first time. Whereas Tesco (www.tesco.co.uk) gives you a CD containing its range to speed up the process, Sainsbury's asks you to wait five minutes while it loads the 'store controller'. Then it downloads the product range. A technological miracle, in its way. You can even ask it to prevent you buying anything that isn't organic or calorie-controlled. But, boy, is it hard work! Still, you can save your list, and next time will be a piece of (Be Good To Yourself) cake.

Organics Direct (www.organicsdirect.co.uk)

An alternative to the supermarket: organic vegetarian produce, as well as beer, wine, clothes, bed linen and nappies, delivered from small farmers to your door. A pleasant site offering a much wider range than you'd expect. But no Bob the Builder pasta shapes.

ARTS, ENTERTAINMENT AND WHAT'S ON

SceneOne (www.sceneone.co.uk)
The Internet used to be a great place to find out what was on at the pictures – in Los Angeles.

Thankfully, things have changed. If you want to know what's on at the cinema locally, you are spoiled for choice. You can go to the cinema company's site, or to a local site such as **thisisgloucestershire.co.uk**. A specialist entertainment listings site, on the other hand, can tell you what's on anywhere, and not only at the cinema. If you are desperate to see *The Godfather*, you'll discover you have to go to Aberystwyth to find it. And it will tell you what you are missing on the television.

SceneOne goes further still. As well as listings of cinema, television, radio, theatre, comedy, music and more, it offers reviews and gossip. The site is clean and easy to read. It is easy to find your way around, but the sliding panels it uses may present problems for older equipment.

The film listings work well. You select your local area, then ask what's on, listed either by film or by cinema. Or you can search the whole site for a film title or anything else. The reviews, cobbled together from the newspapers, are basic memory-joggers.

The site is aimed squarely at the young and the metropolitan, which might put you off. Its Music section consists solely of reviews of pop CDs. Theatre listings dwindle outside Greater London.

And there are strange omissions. The Book section has short, rather childish reviews, but doesn't tell you the price of the book. The excellent television listings allow you to see what's on one channel or all main channels for one day or several. But it doesn't tell you which programmes are repeats.

The Radio listings tell you what pieces are being played on Radio 3, which most newspapers can't manage, but it doesn't really have much to say about local stations.

Useful, then, but you won't be able to throw out your local paper, *Radio Times* or your listings magazines just yet.

All Music Guide (www.allmusic.com)

The All Music Guide is a kind of music encyclopedia, but with entries cunningly cross-referenced to make more of them. If you let it, it'll build you a new record collection in no time.

From its start page, you can browse through style categories or search by artist name, album, song or label. There are also various articles and features to look at, a glossary and a series of 'music maps', which trace the various styles back to their roots. This kind of curatorial attitude to pop music will be familiar to anyone who has ever read American music criticism.

If you look at the pages on individual artists and groups, you will find they carry on this obsessive categorising, with sometimes humorous results. At the end of each artist's biography and before the minutely detailed discography you can use what is called an 'Artist Browser' to find vaguely similar artists. For instance, if you are looking at Bob Dylan, the browser suggests you might like someone 'Lighter, freer', and throws up a picture of Ry Cooder. Nonsense, but well worth the price of admission. You can even join in the process, by filling in a form to say whether you consider Dylan 'Light, Free, Transparent' or 'Dark, Pessimistic, Bitter', among other things. It's a pity the song titles don't link to sound files, but you can't have everything. Yet.

Ain't It Cool News (www.aintitcoolnews.com)

One of the half-dozen most famous websites in the world, this ugly and amateurish assembly of reviews and illicit previews regularly reduces Hollywood to tears. On occasions its Head Geek, Harry Knowles, condemns films before they've even come out of the editing suite. On the other hand, when he loves a film, he really loves it. If you love movies, you will want to bookmark this site.

The Internet Movie Database (www.imdb.com)

A vast database of information about films. If you want to know Beatrice Dalle's real name and what she appeared in before *Betty Blue*, and that film's French title, and her birthplace, and other people from the same town (Alain Robbe-Grillet), this is for you.

GMN.com (www.gmn.com)

The Global Music Network covers classical music and jazz with live 'webcasts', record reviews with samples, and all manner of written information. You must register for the webcasts and tell GMN whether you want RealAudio or Windows Media Player sound.

What's On Stage (www.whatsonstage.com)

Details of theatre, classical music and the performing arts generally around Britain. Offers news, reviews of new shows and secure online ticket booking, with a collection of seating plans to help you select your spot.

Books Unlimited (www.booksunlimited.co.uk)

The *Guardian*'s impressive collection of book-related material, including gossip, reviews, reading lists, poetry, humour and reader participation. The pick of the British online books pages.

Art Guide (www.artguide.co.uk)

Another huge database, this time carrying details of exhibitions and events for lovers of the visual arts and museums. For those of you who don't want to find their own way through them, it offers themed selections, such as 'Fun for Kids' and 'Glorious Eccentrics'. Stylishly done.

Comedy Online (www.comedyonline.co.uk)

Listings, news and interviews about the club comedy scene in Britain. Not exactly stylish, but it does the job.

Days Out (www.virgin.net/daysout)

Virgin Net's listings of events and attractions, searched by typing in details of your target area, preferred activities and time frame. Lots of answers to the perennial question, 'What shall we do with the kids?'

MONEY, PERSONAL FINANCE AND CAREER

This Is Money (www.thisismoney.co.uk)

The web is good for personal finance. Sites can have instant access to changing financial data and can perform complex calculations with ease while you wait for the next page or animation to load. The difficulty is finding one that gets the balance right between comprehensive coverage and sheer overkill.

The *Daily Mail* has had years of experience in these matters, and its site, This Is Money, displays the fruits of that expertise. It is a simple but thorough guide to all the central areas of personal finance that are so hard for most of us to follow: bank accounts, mortgages, pensions, insurance, tax and investments. It does not actively promote personal share trading like some sites, but the guidance is there in case you want it.

A menu gives access to each of the subject areas. When you reach the subject page, a column of headings leads on to articles on topics of current interest. At the side of each page, a toolbox gives you access to the raw facts: interest rates, tax rates, useful calculators and plain-English guides to the technical terms used. The whole site is cleanly designed and simple to navigate, with a few advertisements around the place but none so garish as to prevent you reading the text.

If all that is not enough for you, you can write in and attempt to have your questions answered, although as usual the site makes no guarantee that your query will be dealt with. All in all, a solid, basic site for anyone who wants to read the kind of information you'd get in a newspaper's personal finance pages.

The Motley Fool UK (www.fool.co.uk)

The Motley Fool is an American success story, now transplanted to London and shaking his tickling stick at the stuffier City conventions. The site aims, in its own words, to 'educate, amuse and enrich the individual investor'. Unlikely though it may seem, it certainly manages the middle task of the three. Here's the Fool's explanation of why we all need to take an interest in money which, it readily admits, is 'as dull as the dullest thing in Basingstoke'.

'You have to learn something about it, because otherwise you're not going to be able to keep yourself in Mr Kipling's Jam Tarts and fingerless knitted gloves after you've retired,' he says. Anyway, jokes aside, the Fool is a clown on a mission. And the mission is to overturn the received wisdom of the investment professionals.

To that end, the site offers its Fool's School, a set of simple tutorials in such topics as the basics of share investment and 'How To Read An Annual Report in 5 Minutes'. Elsewhere there is a refreshingly sceptical approach to some of the great City wheezes of our day, from the dotcom companies to derivatives.

And all this carries through to the message boards, which are full of ripe and pithy comment on some of the most hyped companies and stock issues around. The fun on this site does not extend only to the site creators. But beneath all that is a solid selection of company quotes and data that will help you create your own share portfolio and manage it from the site.

Money Guru (www.moneyguru.co.uk)

A much more strait-laced investment site, it includes a 'Guru guide' in a pop-up window, explaining what the site can do for you. Lots of stuff for the casual visitor, but if you pay £11.95 a month you get more detailed information on individual companies and the markets.

ScreenTrade (www.screentrade.co.uk)

This is an online insurance broker, promising 'Instant insurance from the names you know'. True in part, but it depends on your idea of 'instant'. Completing one of its motor insurance proposal forms online is not for those in a hurry or the impatient. But the deals are good.

The Biz (www.thebiz.co.uk)

Confusingly designed but useful directory of links for British businesses. There really is more here than initially meets the eye, but the design does the site no favours.

Financial Times (www.ft.com)

The newspaper of choice for those with a keen interest in money. Excellent if you need to research a publicly listed company. It has a powerful archive search section, but if you go far enough into it you are charged.

E*Trade United Kingdom (www.etrade.co.uk)

These are the people who popularised 'day trading' of shares in the US, and their cut-price rates for conducting business have alarmed more traditional brokers – and made them the number-one online broker in this country.

Blue Square (www.bluesq.com)

While we're on the subject of gambling, this is the unadulterated article, complete with horses jumping over sticks and people knocking balls around. Apparently the first British online betting site, it also offers a range of novelty wagers. It is offering five to one that Ian Beale in *EastEnders* will set up an Internet company by the end of the year.

Job Search UK (www.jobsearch.co.uk)

Huge database of job vacancies across the country and in all manner of industries, new and old. It also allows job seekers to complete their CV in an online form and send it in free. Employers pay to advertise. Not attractive, exactly, but functional.

Monster.co.uk (www.monster.co.uk)
Heavily advertised and slightly flashy online recruitment agency. Does a similar job to Job Search, but has a lot of useful extra material about writing job letters, CVs, networking and so on.

**Money Origami
(http://www.umva.com/~olay/money/boots/)**
If you really want to know what to do with your money, take a look at this.

THE MEDIA: TV, RADIO, NEWSPAPERS AND MAGAZINES

BBC Online (www.bbc.co.uk)
To call the BBC's massive online presence a website is like calling Mexico City a village. The corporation has ploughed masses of licence-fee money into the site in an effort to make itself one of the handful of globally known media names in this new century. Whether it has succeeded or not remains to be seen. Certainly **bbc.co.uk** is very popular and well liked in this country, because it offers something for most tastes, all done with a touch of class. Although a lot of the pages here are linked to television and radio programming, it goes beyond that a lot of the time to create a new experience. And it is not only about 'broadcasting': there are lots of invitations here for you, the viewers and listeners, to join in and have your say.

The opening page, proudly proclaiming itself the UK's favourite website, offers plenty of ways round. There's an A–Z Index and a Search box. There are a handful of featured articles in the centre of the page, then a list of subject categories and regional and departmental home pages on the left.

On the right are links to news and sport, with headline links and icons for video and sound; beneath that, there is a weather panel, offering the forecast for your area; then come links to other BBC online centres; links to live sound feeds from the five BBC Radio channels; and a link to **beeb.com**, the BBC's less convincing commercial website. Elsewhere, there's a drop-down menu that lets you find websites for many (but not all) of the BBC's radio and television programmes and lots more.

Many of these links take you to huge sites in their own right. The News area (**www.news.bbc.co.uk** if you want to go straight there) has a running 'ticker' with the latest headlines across the page, plus links to longer versions of the main stories, some of them with sound and video. As well as straightforward UK news the site covers business, science and technology, health, education, sport and show business. For world news, an 'image map' lets you select the continent you are interested in, and then you go to the start page for, say, Africa. A low-graphics version is always available for those whose browsers and connections are struggling.

There are similarly vast sections for sport, weather, nature, kids and many more, or you may simply choose to go to the support sites for your favourite programmes. I love *Local Heroes*, in which a man on a mountain bike wobbles around the country to find out about famous inventors and redo their experiments using washing-up bottles and string. On its site are instructions for doing some of the experiments, biographies of the scientists and lots more, including videos of viewers making fools of themselves. Be warned: you will need up-to-date plug-ins to use these features.

If radio is your thing, you have to look a bit harder, but there's still plenty to discover, even if it's only an 'interactive map' of Virtual Ambridge. And there I was thinking it was real . . .

CNN.com (www.cnn.com)

The BBC isn't the world's only television news source, as we all discovered in the Gulf War. Sometimes it is interesting to take a different perspective on the world, and here CNN is well worth getting to know. This is another vast site, which starts off looking rather like the BBC online start page but is navigated differently. At the top it's all hard news from the US and the rest of the world, with a lead story, a string of other headlines and links to other categories. But scroll down and things start to soften up and surprise you. First there's a lot of sports and business stories and statistics, then world news, then politics, law, entertainment, health, personal finance, computing, space, nature, travel, food and so on. To get to this stuff, you scroll down and keep scrolling.

Some of the references are slightly comical to our ears ('Some Britons fear country is becoming giant theme park'; 'Proposed "erotic gherkin" riles some Londoners') but occasionally it does us good to see ourselves through others' eyes. These stories come mainly from America's wire services, but occasionally from newspapers in the countries concerned. They are usually equipped with links to take you further – that's the joy of reading stories on the web, as opposed to in, say, *Time* magazine, which is heavily promoted and linked to on this site.

Naturally, there is plenty of video, although as usual the experience is more of a novelty than anything else if you are using your normal home telephone line for Internet access.

RadioTower.com (www.radiotower.com)
Listening to live radio stations from all over the world on your computer is one of the least-known pleasures of the Internet. This is an exceptionally clean and straightforward way to browse the world's radio by country, format or station name. You must have the RealPlayer plug-in for it to work. And you should be on an unmetered connection: it's addictive.

NewsNow (www.newsnow.co.uk)
A British 'news aggregator', meaning a site that brings together lots of current headlines from online sources and

newspapers. If you see anything you are interested in, click on it and the full story pops up. Covers news, business, technology and more. You can also search the last thirty days' headlines. Plus, lots of useful British links.

Paperboy (www.thepaperboy.co.uk)

Contains links to the home pages of more than 300 UK national and local newspapers, but they are not searchable. There is, however, a searchable link to the news agencies Reuters and AP. Also links to the larger US site.

Moreover (www.moreover.com)

The ultimate headline site, bringing in searchable headlines from 1,500 sources. Click from there straight to the main site of whichever worthy organ the story is to be found in.

Ananova (www.ananova.com)

Is Ananova, a computer-generated autocutie, the future of news? Or is she just a silly way of dressing up stories from the Press Association, Britain's venerable news agency? Very *Blade Runner*, but see for yourself.

fish4News (www.fish4news.com)

Constantly updated news from websites belonging to most of Britain's local papers. Click on a link to go to the local site.

Electronic Telegraph (www.telegraph.co.uk)

First and best of the online versions of Britain's newspapers, with an excellent archive for those who register (it's not too painful). The site's search engine is slightly peculiar, but worth persevering with. It does allow you to search the edition of a particular day of a particular month of a particular year, or you can leave any or all of these options blank.

Salon (www.salon.com)

The most celebrated of online magazines, this US product always contains something intriguing, even for those who don't live there. Recently scaled down some sections, but still packs a punch.

Drudge Report (www.drudge.com)
Briefly the most famous Internet operation of them all when it exposed President Clinton's dalliance with Monica Lewinsky. Slightly hard to see what the fuss is about, but you never know what might turn up.

British TV Comedy (www.phill.co.uk)
One of the great things about the Internet is the way it allows all of us to benefit from the labours of the truly obsessed. This is a typically unpolished amateur site that contains a comprehensive archive of every show that ever tried to raise a laugh on this side of the Atlantic. The place to go when you really have to know who played Arthur Mullard's wife in *Yus, My Dear*.

REFERENCE AND OFFICIAL INFORMATION

Open.gov.uk (www.open.gov.uk)
The grand entrance to the British government's vast array of web resources. If you learn to find your way around this lot you should never again have to stand in a queue for a leaflet or spend hours on the telephone waiting to find the person who knows the answer to your query about VAT, children's inoculations or building regulations.

Unfortunately, finding your way around is not as easy as it might be. There are numerous overlapping devices for finding your way to the right site, but some odd decisions have been made. Who would have thought, for example, that the Department for Education and Employment would be listed under 'D', rather than 'E'? Anyway, the alphabetical list of organisations is only one option. There's also a drop-down menu of the big-name sites, beginning with The Monarchy, a list of sites organised by topic, a list of 'what's new' and a list of 'pathfinders', these being the major government 'portals'. And finally there's a search box.

Oddly, while the site conforms to every known standard for legibility and usability, it looks terrible. Fine white type on a blue background in the headings does not help. But that's not the point: this is not a place to linger. Indeed, there's nothing to linger over. It just speeds you straight to the information you need. With so many documents at hand, using the search box is a recipe for disappointment. But if you go to the 'Pathfinders' you can begin to narrow things down. There you find NHS Direct, the National Grid for Learning, the Information Age Champions and all the other snappily titled bureaucracies created by this government. You can also learn from the Public Appointments Directory that 35,000 people currently sit on quangos. A couple of links later and there they are listed by name, from Professor AJ Gray (who comes under A, for some reason) to Professor AJ Zuckerman.

Once you leave the **open.gov.uk** portal and enter the sites themselves, all sorts of designs and navigation systems are used. But that's not the point. Being able to sit down and find everything from the 'Report of the Inquiry Into Hunting With Dogs' to the rules for selling sprouts in kilograms has got to be a boon to the British population. Be aware that some of these links will suddenly trigger your Acrobat plug-in so they can place nice ready-to-print documents on your desktop.

Britannica.com (www.britannica.com)

There are lots of encyclopedia sites on the web, but if you have a grain of patriotism in you most of them will leave you disappointed. The much-praised Encarta (**www. encarta.msn.com**), for instance, had not one word on the English novelist DH Lawrence, although it did manage to find lots of mid-Western civil engineers with similar names. Britannica, however, is the real thing.

For a start, it has the whole text of the vast encyclopedia as it existed in the days when it was sold door to door. That on its own would be the basis for an excellent site, but it also adds a string of useful web links to anything you unearth. And, on top of all that, it has recently been attempting to turn itself into a portal, which means the usual news and features, weather, stocks and shares, sport and even an extensive shopping area, where what may well prove to be the final printed edition of the *Encyclopaedia Britannica* sits there waiting for someone to take it home – a snip at $1,250.

Virtual Reference Desk (www.refdesk.com)

Nothing to look at, this site packs a real punch, because it contains links to every reference tool you can imagine, from Acronym Finder to Homework Help, not to mention 260 search engines. Endless uses.

Your Dictionary (www.yourdictionary.com)

Links to more online dictionaries than you ever imagined possible, covering languages, specialist subjects, dialects and more. Polish up your Navajo, among others.

Bartleby.com (www.bartleby.com)

Electronic books – or e-books – are one of the great resources of the Internet. Bartleby searches and links to a few of the more useful ones.

xrefer (www.xrefer.com)

Styling itself the web's reference engine, this clean and minimal site offers a search box leading to a useful and growing collection of up-to-date reference books from people like Bloomsbury, Macmillan and OUP.

Directory Enquiries (www.bt.com/phonenet.uk)

Fed up with paying through the nose for directory enquiries and then being allowed only a limited look at the results? Use the web version and you can try as many times as you like.

Railtrack (www.railtrack.com)

The timetable is searchable through a prominent link on the opening screen. You can specify starting or arrival times and your route. But you can't buy a ticket. For that you want www.thetrainline.com.

Pitsco's Ask An Expert (www.askanexpert.com)

An American site aimed at schoolchildren, but fun none-theless. You select a category, and then the site provides you with an email address for you to write off with your query. Responses may take a week.

LAW on the WEB (www.lawontheweb.co.uk)

Excellent source of legal information by a British solicitor, including guides to the law, a directory of law firms by speciality and even a review of the most recent episode of *Ally McBeal*. Terrible design, including a plethora of irksome animations, but don't be put off.

Streetmap (www.streetmap.co.uk)

Remarkable instant street maps for the whole of the UK. Search by street name, postcode, place name, grid reference or even telephone area code. For annotated maps including hotels, etc., try **www.multimap.com**. If you want annotated maps and town plans for other countries, try **www.mapquest.com**.

CHILDREN, SCHOOLS AND EDUCATION

CBBC (www.bbc.co.uk/kids)

The CBBC (Children's BBC) area in the massive BBC online site is updated daily and provides the usual reliable balance of entertainment and information.

For the older children, that means pop and celebrities, with the odd animal or dinosaur making an appearance, while the younger ones (with a special Little Kids site of their own) can colour in pictures or send in their own. A selection of nice printable black-and-white line drawings of Postman Pat, Spot, Noddy, Pingu and the latest favourite, Bob the Builder, is available.

Kids can do simple onscreen quizzes, vote and look at sites concerning everything from *The Teletubbies* to *Live and Kicking*. Most have simple Flash-based animated games that take only a matter of minutes to download.

For the Little Kids, these can usually be managed with even the wobbliest of mouse hands, but parents will need to be on hand to give some help with the instructions. Few pre-school kids will benefit from being told to 'make sure you have Java enabled in your browser': or maybe they will . . .

The *Teletubbies* area is particularly well done, with a lot of information for sceptical parents wondering why they speak the way they do, and why Tinky-Winky has a handbag. All your questions – except that one – are answered in a good 'FAQ', and you can sign up for a *Teletubbies* email news if you want more.

The *Blue Peter* site keeps up the old tradition of education and entertainment, although the emphasis on the presenters as teen idols would not have appealed to Christopher Trace and Valerie Singleton. The famous 'Makes' are well represented, including gifts, recipes and outdoor projects.

As on most of the BBC sites, there is an opportunity for feedback through its message boards. They obviously tap into a real need for children to say what they feel. On the day I looked there were 1,700 messages on the subject of Harry Potter.

National Grid For Learning (www.ngfl.gov.uk)
Part of the government's grand plans for wiring the country's classrooms into the Information Superhighway, whatever that is. No one could call this a particularly welcoming site, but it does have masses of information about what goes on in schools, for parents and especially teachers. It also has a lot of information about educational software and CD-ROMs in case you are interested in those. There is also a large and useful section offering advice on taking care of children when they use the Internet.

The site is not the easiest in the world to navigate. Run your mouse over the main central graphic and you will see individual submenus pop up when you touch one of the main headings: schools, further education, libraries, museums and so on. Then you can go straight to any of the headings on the submenu. Schools, for instance, leads to Standards Site, VTC (whatever that is), National Curriculum and so on. There is also a Parents Centre, but it is busy, suggesting a pent-up need that this site does not really address. On the whole, the site suggests a professional establishment that does not really welcome scrutiny from its customers: no concessions are made in the area of jargon, for instance. And a high proportion of the links seem not to work.

On the other hand, all the information you need as a parent is here somewhere. Your best advice is to use the Search Tools provided in the panel on the right-hand side. A search for the learning materials about the environment for instance, to support a primary school project, took me rapidly to the Department of the Environment's own website for children on the subject of global warming. Not the most entertaining site, in fact no fun at all, but an essential bookmark for any family with young children. It could do with a shake-up, however.

Disney UK (www.disney.co.uk)

All the usual Disney stuff here, but if you expect much more than the hard sell for the latest films, merchandise and theme-park attractions you may be disappointed. On the other hand, the trailers for forthcoming movies are great, if you have the QuickTime plug-in.

Pokemon World (www.pokemon.com)

One day the Pokemon craze will fade away, but for the time being this remains perhaps the most visited children's site in the world. But the owners are well aware of that and it loads quickly and securely. There's a complete 'spotters' guide' to the charmless little creatures, lengthy instructions on how to play the game that goes with them, and even entertaining pictures of the world's children dressed up as Pikachu, Squirtle and the rest. Nakedly commercial, but at least all the ads are for the one product.

Ask Jeeves for Kids (www.ajkids.com)
Kids like the AskJeeves idea as much as adults, and they need a search engine. Jeeves is pretty canny, and promises that any link is likely to be safe: of course, kids can always go on from there to something less desirable. The site also offers games, advice and useful suggestions on what to do when you are bored. This is an American site, of course, so some of the references may not make sense to British kids.

National Geographic (www.nationalgeographic.com/kids)
A very jolly site using the vast resources of the great glossy magazine. Taps into children's endless enthusiasm for wild animals, dinosaurs and the like but also offers a few surprises. Plus competitions, cartoons, and the opportunity to correspond with kids around the world.

Learnfree (www.learnfree.co.uk)
Excellent British education site covering everything from choosing a nursery to 16-plus study. Lots of news, features and useful links, plus a 'jargon buster', recipes for kids and even the odd game, but that part of the site requires you to register and download a plug-in.

How Stuff Works (www.howstuffworks.com)
More for the older child, this features excellent straight-forward accounts of how anything and everything works, from computer monitors to teeth. Very well done and largely free of advertising.

Revise It (www.revise.it)
A revision site aimed squarely at the core GCSE subjects. Nicely designed and well focused, the site requires you to register and then gives you access to revision guides, exam timetables, tests, study ideas and discussions.

The Simpsons (www.thesimpsons.com)

One of the best official television spin-offs you are likely to see. The animations work smoothly and the depth of information is remarkable. More than you ever thought it possible to learn about a series of yellow-skinned cartoon suburbanites.

Unofficial Guides (www.unofficial-guides.com)

Directory of some of Britain's universities and colleges, though not as 'frank and fearless' about them as its title might suggest. More relevant information than you'll find in the official prospectuses.

NeoPets (www.neopet.com)

A genuine Internet sensation. Based in Britain, but working hard to disguise that, this site lets you design your own cyberpet and let it live in a virtual world with those created by other visitors. Its very popularity means it is currently difficult to use, but that may change.

TRAVEL AND TRANSPORT

Travelocity (www.travelocity.co.uk)

A huge travel 'portal' with masses of information and instantaneous quotes for fares, hotels, car hire and more.

First you are expected to register, a slightly tedious process requiring you to cough up your name, address and email and invent a username and password. The advantage, however, is that you can now book things straight from the site, using the lengthy search forms. Even then, you will need your wits about you. A search for a hotel near one airport managed to come up with a list that began with one 140 miles away – but that was because it was the cheapest, and I had specified that I wanted them ordered by price.

It will also search for package holidays, wrapping up information supplied by **www.bargainholidays.com**. When you have found one that meets your requirements, you can ask for confirmation of its availability, which is emailed to you. Or you can telephone Bargain Holidays' call centre, if you still use the old technology. There is a basic resort guide for each destination, telling you the local currency, an up-to-date weather forecast and a modest amount of tourist information. A separate page takes you straight to last-minute bargains starting this weekend, gathered from the computers of nearly thirty tour companies.

For much of its information the site links to its US parent and to outside providers, but be aware that these pages will assume you are travelling from America. You can also find a photo and video gallery about some destinations, currency converters and much more.

All in all, a bright, easy-to-use round-up of what's available in travel and holidays for the casual traveller. If you just want to see what is available from your local airport on any given weekend, this sort of site does the job very well. You might compare Microsoft's equivalent, Expedia (www.expedia.co.uk), which has many of the same features and a very similar look, and features destination information by the Rough Guides.

Lonely Planet (www.lonelyplanet.com)

For those who think the Rough Guides are soft, Lonely Planet offers advice and information for the serious backpacker. But it is also a clear, elegantly designed travel resource for those of us who prefer more conventional holidays. The destination pages, rehashed from the books, are assisted by recent reports from travellers, some of them in wild disagreement and none of them verified by the Lonely Planet team.

Work from a comprehensive site search engine on the start page, or point your mouse at a map on the destinations page. Another interesting feature is the 'Theme Guides', which allow you to choose 'Music' or 'Beaches' as your starting point and let the guides' staff select some suitable destinations around the world. These change monthly.

In the meantime, the Lonely Planet bulletin board, 'The Thorn Tree', has established itself as a good place for travellers to exchange information, advice and tall tales. You can read these, but you will have to register to join in. 'What is actually a koala?' asks someone. 'Is it an Australian dish?'

Then there's a huge area for travel news, collected from mainstream news sources around the world, and a huge selection of 'postcards' from travellers, full of quirky advice and recommendations. The travel health section is almost a site in its own right, covering everything from gippy tummy to blistered feet.

Refreshingly, Lonely Planet has resisted the urge to turn its undoubted pulling power over to the advertisers. There are no ads on the pages, and even the propaganda for its own products is sparse. The result is a site that loads quickly and easily and is eminently legible.

Cheapflights.com (www.cheapflights.co.uk)

A very straightforward site, specialising in flight-only bookings. Select your destination and the site goes straight to a list of starting airports and prices. Then it tells you how to contact the travel agent or bucket shop making the offer. There are a few trimmings, but that's about it, except for a useful system for sending you an email alert when a fare falls below a price you specify.

Ebookers (www.ebookers.com)

More flight and hotel searching facilities. Ebookers uses a step-by-step system to take you through the process from initial enquiry to purchase, which you can do online. It does not handle package holidays.

Rough Guide Travel (www.roughguides.com)

If you know the books, you'll know what to expect. Search by country or city and go straight to the full text of the original guidebook, augmented by travellers' discussion areas, special features and new information. The only area that is under par is the 'travel center' (sic), which is just a page of ads from Rough Guides' 'travel partners'.

UK Public Transport Information (www.pti.org.uk)
Not the most exciting site, but, for those of us who mainly travel around Britain, this would appear to have everything. It offers links to both online rail and coach timetables, ferries, internal flights and lots more.

The Trainline.com (www.thetrainline.com)
Highly publicised site offering price comparisons and online booking for all the British railway companies. Register, type in the details of your journey, and the mysteries of the ticket pricing system are laid bare in seconds.

RAC Route Planner (www.rac.co.uk/services/routeplanner)
If you don't have something similar on your computer, try the RAC's online route planner. It is highly used, so don't be surprised if you have a long wait, but it's worth it. Great detail, including a map, distances, times and details of current roadworks en route. Something similar is available from the AA: www.theaa.com/motoringandtravel/routes.

Railroad Subway and Train Maps (http://pavel.physics/sunysb.edu/RR/maps.html)
Wouldn't it be nice to have a map of the local underground railway system in your pocket when you next arrive in Baku, Azerbaijan? Or in Bucharest or Buenos Aires? They're all here, along with some 322 other transport maps. Another priceless resource from the world's obsessives.

AA Where to Stay, Where to Eat (www.theaa.co.uk/hotels)
National listings and search engine for hotels, bed-and-breakfast, pubs and restaurants. When you find somewhere you fancy, it will provide you with a map or a detailed route plan.

FUN, GAMES, SPORTS AND THE VERY PECULIAR

Meriweather's Flight Deck Simulations (www.meriweather.com/flightdeck.html)

Do you ever catch a glimpse of the flight deck in an Airbus and wonder what all those knobs and levers actually do? Jerome Meriweather, who is a website expert for United Airlines, has put together a virtual flight deck on the web. I have included it here as a good example of the kind of thing that only the web can do, and also because it is a one-man private project done in Jerome's spare time.

It's not a flight simulator, but a kind of educational tool. First you select from one of four planes – three Boeings and an Airbus. Then you have to select how you would like the flight deck displayed, either with a menu down one side or without. Then you run your mouse over the whole picture and menus appear to tell you what the various parts are: overhead maintenance panel, centre instrument panel and control pedestal. Clicking on one, say the centre instrument panel, brings up a much larger cutout of just that section. Now you can click on each element in turn to see what it does.

It would not be true to say that this stuff arrives on your screen very quickly: the graphics are too complicated for that. But when they do arrive they are all well presented and clearly labelled. The problem comes in following the labelling. It's one thing to be told that something is for ILS information and quite another to understand what that means. Actually, Meriweather has anticipated that: there's a glossary elsewhere on the site, plus a check list of cockpit procedures before take-off and a series of brilliant, virtual-reality, 360-degree pictures of the flight decks of everything from the Apollo lunar module to a B–17 Flying Fortress. You will need the QuickTime plug-in for these.

None of this will equip you to fly a plane, of course. But it's typical of the ability of the web to let people bring their personal enthusiasms to a worldwide audience that can take them or leave them. One day I will want to know what one of those flight-deck switches does, and I will know where to come.

The Onion (www.theonion.com)

The Onion began life as an old-fashioned printed magazine, but now that the rest of the world can read it online it has taken on a new life.

Naughtily billing itself as 'America's Finest News Source', it offers a minutely detailed parody of the American style of journalism as practised by *USA Today* in particular. Stories such as 'Spouse Under Fire For Telling Anecdote Wrong' and 'Lanthanum Quits Periodic Table of Elements ("The world of chemistry was shaken Monday by lanthanum's announcement that the popular 57th element will quit Transition Group IIIb of the periodic table at the end of the summer")' are coupled with statistical graphics telling us, for instance, 'Where Daddy Keeps His Gun'. The answer, by the way, being a close tie between 'With Uncle Jeb until Daddy gets paroled' and 'Against Mommy's head'.

The stories on its newspaper-style front page are carried on at greater length inside, many of them reaching great heights of satirical exaggeration. Elsewhere, though, *The Onion* turns into something resembling a real magazine, with interviews, reviews, columns, quizzes, cartoons and all the rest. Well, the anonymous satire is better, but it may not be to everyone's taste. It is also not for the under-eighteens, because of the language.

In the same vein, take a look at tvgohome (**www. tvgohome.com**), Britain's best online humour effort. A single fortnightly page parodying the listings in the *Radio Times*, it takes a few swipes at television on its way to satirising the whole British way of life. Thrill to 'Indiana Jones and the Doomed Office Romance' ('the former adventurer has turned his back on the world of death-defying peril in favour of the quiet life of a Swinton Insurance call-centre manager'). Marvel at 'Disraeli Nights: Erotic drama starring David Seaman as Tory politician Benjamin Disraeli . . . Contains improper language, ankles, full-frontal nudity, sideburn clutching and goal kicks.' Again, be warned that the language and content are not intended for children.

Funny.co.uk (www.funny.co.uk)

An extensive collection of comedy and humour links on the web. It also carries jokes and a forum for discussions on comedy topics, although sadly unfrequented. Not funny, but useful.

Humor Database (www.humordatabase.com)

A very large list of jokes and humorous lists of the sort that keep popping up in your email. You can even search for the Top 30. They are all labelled with 'PG'-type ratings.

Wireplay (www.wireplay.com)

As an introduction to the world of online computer gaming, take a look at this site. To do that, you have to have CDs of the latest games already and be prepared to download the software to permit you to play online. But Wireplay has a few Java-type games you can play from the site, as well as a shop to buy CD games. For more general news and information about games, try Gamespot (www.gamespot.com).

Football365 (www.football365.com)

Enthusiastic and blokeish football site holding all the latest news, gossip and comment. Predictably, it rather loses interest when you drop out of the Premiership. But the tone of voice will be right for many people. A more serious newsy note is struck by Soccernet (www.soccernet.com).

CricInfo (www.cricket.org)

Whereas there are any number of well-matched soccer sites, it is generally agreed that CricInfo justifies its claim of being 'The home of cricket on the Internet'. It offers scorecards refreshing every ninety seconds, constantly updated reports and even live commentary using Real-Audio. Behind that lies a huge volume of material on clubs and competitions, right down to the grass roots.

Planet Rugby (www.planet-rugby.com)

Very lively site for Rugby Union enthusiasts. Or try the rival Scrum (www.scrum.com), which favours a cleaner look and a less excitable tone of voice.

Stick Figure Death Theatre (www.sfdt.com)

Lovingly created animations featuring the last moments of sundry stick men, sometimes with musical accompaniment. Strangely addictive.

Air Sickness Bags Virtual Museum (www.airsicknessbags.com)

Exactly what it says, and much, much more. At least 370-carefully photographed airsickness bags from around the world, plus space sickness bags, sea sickness bags and 'unidentified bags'. So expert is proprietor Steven J Silberberg that there are only three of those. And guess what: he's never been outside the USA – and he's single.

Kiss This Guy (www.kissthisguy.com)

Named after a line in Jimmy Hendrix's 'Purple Haze', this is an archive of misheard lyrics. Currently there are about 1,800 of them for your perusal.

Paul's Radio Museum (www.paulplu.demon.co.uk)

Who would not thrill to find 'A small collection of UK & GDR sets built in the 30s, 40s, 50s and 60s'? Who would not wish to hear again the sounds of Radio Caroline, Radio England and Radio 390, brought to you by the miracle of RealAudio? Oh, well, please yourself.

The Gallery of Regrettable Foods
(www.lileks.com/institute/gallery)

Anyone doubting that we eat better than we did a few years ago should take a trip to this gallery, featuring the glorious products of America's industrial food producers in the recipe books they themselves produced. Brilliantly presented on screen and written up for maximum comic effect.